I0104528

Quakers and the Search for Peace

edited by Sharon Hoover

Friends Publishing Corporation
Philadelphia, Pennsylvania

Quakers and the Search for Peace

©2010 Friends Publishing Corporation. All rights reserved.

Cover Design: Rachel J. Cox

Printed in the United States of America. No part of this book may be used or reproduced in any manner whatsoever without written permission except in the case of quotations of 200 words or less.

For information contact Friends Publishing Corporation, 1216 Arch Street, Ste. 2A, Philadelphia, PA 19107, or email at <info@friendsjournal.org>.

ISBN: 978-0-9779511-1-6

Contents

Foreword

This volume of articles has been culled from the FRIENDS JOUR-
NAL issues over the last 50-plus years, although the tendency is
toward the more recent.

The completion of this anthology required a good number of steps.
First, various generations of interns dating back to 2002 assembled relevant
articles on various themes, including this one. Then, in the summer of
2009, interns Allison Butler, Constance Grady, Lily Megaw, and Scott
Yorko completed work on a set of preliminary articles and alternates for
this anthology. In early 2010, I, Sharon Hoover, reassembled them into a
coherent collection. That same year, interns Casey Jackson and Meghan
Flynn and volunteer Patty Quinn thoroughly proofread the selected
articles and bridge material. Another 2010 intern, Nicole Gravlin, for-
matted the articles into InDesign and participated in the final editing.

As I read and reread the material, it became clear to me that the search
for peace among Friends began and continues as a spiritual search, not
a political one. The statement by New Zealand Friends focused my
thinking that a search for peace should begin as soon as possible in life
and continue throughout our growing and developing years. "Bless the
little children and forbid them not . . . ," Jesus said. Friends' search for
peace began with such texts as the Sermon on the Mount, not on political
schemes, and we should keep that spiritual basis foremost in our minds.

Today, the Religious Society of Friends is made up of those from the
newborn to the very elderly, from the "birthright" to the recently "convinced," from "attenders" to members. This volume ought to speak to
all of them and to their melding. Based on my own experience of seeing
young Friends contributing enormous strength to the Religious Society
of Friends and to the search for peace, I also decided that it ought to
represent the efforts of Friends of all ages.

There were so many excellent articles that I had to select the final
ones based on representation, sometimes on length in order to include
a great number and variety of articles, and on focus. Articles worked
best with one focus.

I was overcome with riches.

Some articles I tried to keep, and did until the last cut, such as a touching one about a World War I conscientious objector, one on genocide, and one on a disagreement with the direction of Friends' peace seeking. I hope that readers will turn to old JOURNALS for more reading in any area that interests them. And, that they will continue to write articles that will take the ideas of those presented here further into the search for the peaceable kingdom.

S.H.

Introduction

The History of the Peace Testimony

After Henry VIII broke with Rome, he had the Bible published in Early Modern English, the first authorized Bible in vernacular English. The book was quite large and unwieldy, over 14 inches tall. It was meant to be placed in every parish church. In the 15th century, several translations of the Bible, or parts of the Bible, appeared in English. However, in the growing controversies between the crown and its governing entities and the rising separatist sects, many men became martyrs for translating the Bible or for assisting in the effort to put a vernacular Bible into the hands of ordinary people. Finally, in the latter half of the 16th century, the Geneva Bible was written and printed in Geneva, Switzerland, in a size many ordinary people could buy and handle. It was the Bible that John Knox, John Calvin, and the Puritans used in study and writings. The Puritans and their Bible were not favored by Queen Elizabeth I or by King James I, so Elizabeth and James each authorized their own Bibles. The large Bishops' Bible produced under Elizabeth never became popular, but the edition of 1611 that we know as The King James Bible was soon popular throughout the English-speaking world, except among Puritans who continued to favor the Geneva Bible.

The invention of movable type in the 16th century, combined with legally being able to own and to read a Bible in English, unloosed the energy of the Reformation and the European Renaissance into England. Protestants were expected to learn to read in order to read the Bible. As it was the only book most people had, they read and reread it. It was long and complex; it could withstand much reading. People could read and learn from it themselves and know that Jesus did not take up arms against Rome and that he showed and taught people how to serve their neighbors who suffered from religious, social, and economic prejudice. He taught that everyone is a neighbor and that we should show kindness to each one, giving attention and substance to decrease the affliction or sorrow of others.

Fox and early Friends were affected not only by their reading of the

Bible and their search for spiritual Truth, but also by the chaotic political and social times in which they lived. The new and simpler printing presses meant that all sorts of tracts and speeches could be easily disseminated among the people. Thomas Carlyle, an acclaimed Scottish historian and essayist, said that "He who first shortened the labor of copyists by device of movable types was disbanding hired armies, and cashiering most kings and senates, and creating a whole new democratic world . . ."(Sartar Resartus Bk. I, Ch. 5).[1] During and just after the English Civil War, Fox had great hope for the Commonwealth as a new beginning for England's religious and secular order, but he found instead that one kind of dictatorship had merely replaced another. War and killing had not led to the kingdom of God on Earth. At the same time, Friends were accused by people around Oliver Cromwell, then around Charles II, of being "plotters and fighters." It seems an obvious step for Friends to make a stand against the use of arms: "A Declaration from the Harmless & Innocent People of God called Quakers" (1660). They could base their conviction on their experience of the recent war and its aftermath as well as on the teachings and behavior of Jesus, who said, "Love your enemies."

Until the fourth century, when Constantine was emperor of the Roman Empire, Christianity had been pacifist. Also, over the hundreds of years after Constantine, numerous groups of Christian pacifists had developed in Europe.[2] Friends had also, unaware, stepped into a long line of non-Christian pacifists from the time of the Jains in India in the sixth century

---

[1]Those interested in learning about the many different groups and developments that sprang up in 17th century England would do well to read a book by the historian Christopher Hill: *The World Turned Upside Down* (1972). The book is not overly long, and although it is a comprehensive history, it is quite readable. John Punshon's *Portrait in Grey* (1984), an important book in Quaker history and theology, gives a short history of the time as it relates to his interpretation of Fox's thought.

[2]Peter Brock has written the most definitive history of pacifists in Europe, *Pacifism in Europe to 1914* (1972). He also has a small, very readable overview of pacifism that many people will want to read: *Varieties of Pacifism: A Survey from Antiquity to the Outset of the Twentieth Century* (1999).

B.C.E.[3] Today Friends work closely with members of the Church of the Brethren (begun in Germany in 1708) and the Mennonites (founded by the Swiss in the early 16th century). In addition, many contemporary Friends study Buddhism and Zen, major Eastern religions dating back to the years before Jesus. Friends now cooperate with Christian, non-Christian, and secular national and international groups dedicated to a war-free world and to nonviolent ways to solve conflicts.

Friends as a group have adhered to the pacifist tradition since the time of Fox, although some young men, and some young women, have served in uniform. There were times when anyone who served as a combatant was "read out of meeting." Some Friends' meetings, especially more recently, have not rejected those who would use arms but have instead held them in loving concern. Today, there are even groups of Friends who have given outright approval to their young people who serve the nation with arms. The latter Friends are not represented in this anthology.

Friends' experience with pacifism cannot be expressed in categorical terms. Many times the lines between being a pacifist and a non-pacifist have been murky or dangerous. Early seamen, many of whom were Quakers (there were numerous seamen in early England and America), were often bound to follow their captain who might be bound to the monarch or the government to fight back if attacked on the sea. Or if a Quaker owned his own boat, he might be bound to let the queen or king use it in war or to suffer its loss. That could be a difficult choice for a man brought up on the sea with no other obvious way to make a living, especially if he were blacklisted and had a family to support. Where and how one draws a line between cooperating in "war," including undeclared war, has never been easy.

Another difficulty arose when someone called by the monarch or government to bear arms could pay someone else to serve in his stead. Or, he might be able to pay a penalty to the government. The question then arose: "Is providing for another to bear arms simply bearing arms oneself, once removed?" Some Friends chose to pay for a substitute; oth-

---

[3] Karen Armstrong's book *The Great Transformation: The Beginning of our Religious Traditions* (2007) is a fine presentation of the appearance of pacifist religious leaders just before and including Jesus. Reading it, one learns that several of today's great world religions have much in common.

ers refused to do this and went to prison. In the 20th century some men refused conscientious objector status. One might decide that becoming a farmer or a practical nurse in an institution released another man to fight, and that was still cooperating in sending men to kill other men, and increasingly in modern times, to kill women and children. Prison time has also been meted out to many who were judged by officials as not truly conscientious objectors.

If earlier Friends refused to pay for a substitute to go to war or to pay levies for war, their property could be "entailed," that is, fines imposed, often quite large ones. Government officials might take a person's house, furniture, animals, and land. They probably also sent the owner to prison. There was no way to retrieve confiscated property. Money makes war possible. For some years, Friends gave the monarch money saying that it was a gift for the monarch's use. The monarch was then responsible for how it was spent; the thought being that the spending of it was on his or her conscience.

America operated along more democratic lines, even in provincial times. Friends were permitted to participate in government, and in Pennsylvania, they dominated the Assembly for many years. However, when pressed by the people for the Assembly to vote for taxes to protect the settlers, most Friends (not all) resigned from the Assembly rather than to vote on taxes for war. When taxes began to include money for military actions "in the mix," that made not paying for war even more difficult. Friends have never resisted paying taxes to support the operation of peaceful government concerns, but they have looked for ways to separate the taxes spent for war and those for peaceful purposes. During the Vietnam War, a telephone tax was levied expressly for the war, so many Friends refused to pay it. The issue of paying taxes for war has become more and more agonizing for Friends as the United States now maintains a continual, growing, and expensive war-making machine. And, to further confound contemporary Friends, they realize that saving or investing for the future or buying goods for the present supports corporations that have contracts, however small, with the Pentagon. By extension, then, Friends are cooperating in war-enmeshed production and financial systems. The same dilemma faces Friends who work in many industries. The issues of dealing with "war taxes" and providing money to maintain a war economy is an ongoing problem.

Related Prison Work

Early Friends were often sent to prison in England and America for preaching in public, visiting prisoners, refusing to take oaths, or because they acted contrary to one of the many acts that Parliament, the crown, or the provincial government designed to control and to punish them. During the 17th century, many Quakers died in prison and many, many others were crippled or suffered broken health after prison, possibly because they had also been whipped, dragged through the streets, or tortured in some other way before being thrown into prison. Not all Friends or other prisoners suffered such inhumane treatments, but many did, and all who went to prison quickly learned through personal experience that the prisons were rank and without food, water, or sanitation. They were also filled with prisoners whose sentences were long. Many died or went insane. Full of their faith, Friends held meetings in prisons, shared their food, nursed the ill, and after they left, continued to visit and to serve prisoners. They also worked to reduce punishments and to improve prison conditions.

Over the years, this work grew to concern for education for prisoners and especially, more recently, in developing ways for people to live nonviolently, whether in or out of prison. For example, prisoners at Greenhaven Correctional Facility in New York State, in 1975, asked Friends to help them to develop a program for learning to live more peaceably. Out of that request has grown an international program called the Alternatives to Violence Program. Based at first on ideas from the Children's Creative Response to Conflict program and the nonviolent training of the Civil Rights and Vietnam eras, it now is a well-developed program present in many prisons, communities, and schools across the United States and throughout the world, especially in places where personal and community trauma has been great.

"The Peace Testimony" Today

Like the first Friends, Friends today seek spiritual peace within, then in their actions toward others and the world itself. From a well-tended spiritual center, Friends seek to sow peace wherever they go. Many have found themselves called to witness for peace in specific ways in their families, their meetings, their communities, their nation, and their world. From the beginning of the Friends' attention to the conditions of conflict, they have been concerned, not only with arms in war, but in the necessities and characteristics of policing. And like the first Friends, if they are called to civil disobedience, they cooperate with the authorities and continue to be peaceful with their neighbors. They go forward, willing to suffer for their commitment to peace, even as early Friends and Jesus taught and exemplified.

The following statement by New Zealand Friends sits squarely in the context presented above. As Fox and his Friends wrote a declaration for their time, place, and particular situation, so do Friends write declarations to speak to today's challenges.

—*Sharon Hoover*

May 1–15 1987

Rejecting the Clamor of Fear: A Statement from New Zealand Friends

The following is an extract from a statement issued in January 1987 by New Zealand Yearly Meeting:

We totally oppose all wars, all preparation for war, all use of weapons and coercion by force, and all military alliances: no end could ever justify such means. We equally and actively oppose all that leads to violence among people and nations, and violence to other species and to our planet.

We are not naïve or ignorant about the complexity of our modern world and the impact of sophisticated technologies, but we see no reason whatsoever to change or weaken our vision of the peace that everyone needs in order to survive and flourish on a healthy, abundant Earth. [It] is our conviction that there is that of God in everyone, which makes each person too precious to damage or destroy. While someone lives, there is always the hope of reaching that of God within: such hope motivates our search to find nonviolent resolution of conflict. Peacemakers are also empowered by that of God in them. Our individual human skills, courage, endurance, and wisdom are vastly augmented by the power of the loving Spirit that connects all people.

Refusal to fight with weapons is not surrender. We are not passive when threatened by the greedy, the cruel, the tyrant, the unjust. We will struggle to remove the causes of impasse and confrontation by every means of nonviolent resistance available. There is no guarantee that our resistance will be any more successful or any less risky than military tactics. At least our means will be suited to our end. If we seem to fail finally, we would still rather suffer and die than inflict evil in order to save ourselves and what we hold dear. If we succeed, there [will be] no loser or winner, for the problem that led to conflict will have been resolved in a spirit of justice and tolerance. Such a resolution is the only guarantee that there will be no further outbreak of war when each side has regained strength.

The context in which we take this stand is the increasing level of violence around us: child abuse; rape; wife-battering; street assaults; riots; video and television sadism; silent economic and institutional violence; the prevalence of torture; the loss of freedom; sexism, racism, and colonialism; the terrorism of both guerrillas and government soldiers; and the diversion of vast resources of funds and labor from food and welfare to military purposes. But above and beyond all this is the insane stockpiling of nuclear weapons, which could in a matter of hours destroy everyone and everything that we value on our planet.

We must start with our own hearts and minds. Wars will stop only when each of us is convinced that war is never the way. The places to begin acquiring skills and maturity and generosity to avoid or to resolve conflicts are in our own homes, our personal relationships, our schools, our workplaces, and wherever decisions are made. We must relinquish the desire to own other people, to have power over them, and to force our views onto them. We must own up to our own negative side and not look for scapegoats to blame, punish, or exclude. We must resist the urge towards waste and the accumulation of possessions. Conflicts are inevitable and must not be repressed or ignored but worked through painfully and carefully. We must develop the skills of being sensitive to oppression and grievances, sharing power in decision-making, creating consensus, and making reparation. In speaking out, we acknowledge that we ourselves are as limited and as erring as anyone else. When put to the test, we each may fall short.

We do not have a blueprint for peace that spells out every step towards the goal that we share. In any particular situation, a variety of personal decisions could be made with integrity. We may disagree with the views and actions of the politician or the soldier who opts for a military solution, but we still respect and cherish the person. What we advocate is not uniquely Quaker but human and, we believe, the will of God. Our stand does not belong to Friends alone—it is yours by birthright. Together, let us reject the clamor of fear and listen to the whisperings of hope.

Seeking Peace at Home and School

In the first article in the anthology, Kathleen Fisher tells a court how, from her childhood, she developed her religious conviction that killing and other kinds of violence are destructive, showing us the importance of teaching peace from the youngest ages. She also points out that the action she took at the School of the Americas was not a political one; rather, "it was a call of the Spirit that led me across the line." Such an act of civil disobedience may result in a six-month prison term, depending on the particular court and the political climate of the time. Kathleen was cooperative with the court and willing to undergo any punishment. She was walking in the footsteps of early Friends.

Parents and children are often faced with incidents or occasions that present choices regarding war and its glorification. Guiding children is a constant movement of teaching and letting go, always an improvisation that takes consistent attention and prayer. In "Bluebirds for Peace," we read of a parent-child dance that led to a beautiful performance for peace carried out by elementary school children.

No one knows how many Friends are schoolteachers but it is many. For a few years, one yearly meeting held a weekend session for teachers each year where they could pray, share, learn, and weep together. Teaching is a demanding profession, calling on every skill, experience, and personal strength a teacher has, and weekends are usually as full as weekdays. Nevertheless, many teachers availed themselves of the weekend workshops. It would be an impossible dream for most teachers to have a year's sabbatical. Susan Gelber Cannon was fortunate, and we are fortunate that she shares with us insights from her year's sabbatical. These insights may give readers a larger perspective about learning in order to teach more effectively in daily school and in First-day (Sunday) school. They may also encourage more teachers to share peace activities with one another.

The teenaged years are when, as the idiom would have it, "the fat hits the fire." Teenagers can be calm one minute and explosive the next. Teens literally work at a child's level one minute and at an adult level another. An administrator dreads the fight that breaks out anywhere on school grounds. The causes are multiple: from simple muscular, hormonal, metabolic and brain development to immature emotional responses to all the pressures and confusions they feel at home and in their wider cultures. The adults have difficult roles to play, too. They must remember at all times, even in embarrassing or volatile circumstances, that they must act like sensible adults, ones that should be emulated. Stressful is too easy a word to apply to many occurrences in high schools. Fenna Mandolang experienced stress in her large, urban, mixed-race middle school. In her meeting, Friends had guided Fenna to participate meaningfully in Meeting for Worship and business meetings and to take responsibilities along with adults in meeting and yearly meeting activities. She had learned among Friends that she was an important part of any community to which she belonged and that she had a responsibility to cooperate in that community to make it better. She had also been learning among and with the help of adult Friends to become a leader. Her article is one example of what older Friends can teach young Friends to do.

Lawrence Lee points out in his article that another responsibility of meetings is to advise young people about the responsibilities that will come to them concerning their participation in war. At the time Lee wrote, Friends were primarily concerned about young men and the draft. However, boys and girls both, in peace and wartimes, should learn about making a spiritual statement concerning war. This is especially true for those who are certain that they will be pacifists. In addition, young and middle-aged adults must face the fact that draft proposals that have currently been prepared in case of war are now specifying that people of any age can be drafted if they have needed skills. And, in addition, the more pacifist statements that Friends publish, the more seriously they may be taken in the world. Also, as we will see in Kathleen Fisher's article, pacifist statements may be used effectively in places other than in facing a draft board. If one has occasion to give a personal peace testimony in public, it is best to be prepared early.

The final two articles are especially pertinent in the early 21st century: "You, Too, Can Rein in Military Recruiters in the High School" and "ROTC Revisited." Friends would do well to learn the legal and persuasive aspects of these programs. Many students coming out of high school today see no way to get an education, to find a job, or perhaps even to find a place to live. The military service offers them a place to belong after high school, three meals, perhaps some education, as well as a suit to be proud of—it's a great equalizer. The military also gives them an employer to be proud of—a powerful democratic country. ROTC, too, provides high school students with discipline and pride as they serve in ways that often bring them praise in the school and community, and it gives them a step up when they join the active military. Friends could become a presence in school with information set up beside the recruiters and placed in the guidance office. They can also withdraw their own children from receiving military-related mail. We must respect and respond to the needs that encourage young people to join ROTC or the armed forces, and we should present them with choices.

S.H.

Court Testimony of Kathleen Fisher

*March 10, 2000, before Judge Hugh Lawson in U.S. District Court,
Columbus, Ga.: United States of America vs. Kathleen D. Fisher*

Your Honor, I believe that this trial is about the charge of "un-
lawful reentering of a U.S. military reservation and intending
to engage in partisan political activities." Had the arraignment
charge said unlawful reentering alone, I would have pleaded guilty. But
during the funeral procession I was not engaged in "partisan political
activities." For me, crossing the line was a part of a lifelong journey of
spiritual discernment.

I grew up in an evangelical Christian household where I learned
simple truths. "Thou shalt not kill." "Thou shalt not covet anything
that is your neighbor's."

Later I attended a Christian university, where I majored in biology and
studied the Bible. I learned from the prophet Amos how the rich defraud
the poor, crush the needy, and annihilate the peasants of the land. Micah
spoke about beating swords into plowshares and how God requires us
only to do justice, to love goodness, and to walk modestly with God.

At graduate school while studying molecular biology, I had my first
encounter with the Mennonites, a peace church. I learned the intersec-
tion of faith and nonviolence. My understanding of "Thou shalt not
kill" grew. No one is allowed to kill, not even the government.

But my real education came while I worked as a volunteer for the
Mennonite Central Committee. In Swaziland I taught at a school for
refugees, most of whom were from South Africa. After Zimbabwean
independence, I was asked to help rebuild a school and a hospital in Zim-
babwe. There I taught high school and organized the hospital laboratory
and x-ray departments. From my students I learned how faith, vision,
and compassion sustain people in the face of institutional violence, like
apartheid, corporate plunder of their environment, and military oppression through mass murders and other violence. Their example challenged
me to confront injustice in a nonviolent way.

It was in southern Africa where I met two other groups who have shaped my faith in the last 20 years: the Quakers, who speak of "that of God" in everyone, and the Grail, an organization of 2,000 women who each day live out their faith and vision by working globally for change—for social justice, for environmental sustainability, and for celebrating each of our cultures and beliefs. From these two communities I have learned about listening to the hum of creation that is under everything, that we must be as compassionate as God, and that the sword is always beaten by the Spirit. And it is from these two communities that I learned about spiritual discernment and knew that I must let my life speak for my beliefs.

Currently I work for the United States Grail as national staff/networker. Each week I volunteer at the local AIDS hospice and sing in Aurora Chorus, a women's choir that sings "in harmony for peace." I attend Quaker meeting and attempt to lead a life following the Quaker tenets of living in simplicity, choosing a path of nonviolence, and finding "that of God" in everyone. I provide financial assistance for my mother and my older disabled sister. My mother lives with the challenges of aging and heart failure in addition to caring for my sister, who is unable to live independently.

I do have, as all of us do, political opinions. I believe that the School of the Americas represents all that needs changing in U.S. foreign policy and that the closing of the SOA is only a start in reassessing and redirecting U.S. foreign policy. But it was a call of the Spirit that led me across the line. I responded to "that of God" within me by carrying a coffin in honor of the dead: men, women, and children who were the victims of violence.

February 1, 1978

Bluebirds for Peace

by Sandy Eccleston

Most elementary school children fear, as much as they fear anything, being freaks. A child suspects, even when very young, that she is really quite different from all her peers, but she keeps that to herself. (And there is a long existential walk from that secret knowing to the understanding that, whatever our apparent differences, we are all One.) Most people—especially children—try to stay camouflaged. A child is irritated, and sometimes mortified, by the telltale mark that gives her away, whether a crossed eye or a cowlick—no matter how much inward delight she takes in knowing that no one else in the whole world has, has had, or ever will have a thumb print exactly like hers. A child is embarrassed and often angry when a family pattern makes her stand out among her peers. It is years before she really believes that each family has quirks and foibles as painful to its children as her own: a limit of two TV programs from a severely limited list, a rule that older siblings escort younger ones to school, a habit of filling lunch boxes with queer vegetarian concoctions, a red house in a neighborhood of white ones.

Parents love their children, and do not want to humiliate them, do not want to strip the protective covering off the frail egos. At the same time, parents are responsible for nurturing in their children's beings the values they hope will flourish there. To nurture the God-seed in our children requires love and discipline and, as any parent who has ever toilet-trained a child knows, a terrific sense of timing. When to weed? to water? to prune? to stake the child to a family principle, while all the crows of contemporary culture caw in her ears?

Making these decisions and interventions exhausts me. Being a mother is the most grueling discipline I've ever attempted, and—by far—the most satisfying to my spirit. (Some decisions must be made on the spot, without hesitation or prayer, trusting in the Light. But, often, the decisions can wait upon contemplation and insight.) For years now, I have been living with the tensions between my values and the values of the culture. I tense up at another level when I feel the strain in my children, stretched between their love for us and their longing to be like everybody else.

"Everybody else" eats junk food, strives to win, pushes to be first in line, fights back, studies to get the best grades, keeps away from people who are poor, plays with guns and Barbie dolls, believes TV commercials, and keeps so busy with clubs and lessons and visiting everybody else that she doesn't know how to be alone. This is not the life I hope for my children, but this is my children's real world. For a few more years I can keep them snug and close among friends and Friends, but not forever.

The longer I insulate them from the world, the likelier it will seem like forbidden fruit. Even more treacherous, they may begin to believe that it is not the food which is unhealthy, or the competition which is divisive, or the values which are destructive, but the "other people" who are "bad." Children yearn for clear-cut definitions, for "good folks" and "bad folks." If I quarantine my children, they could grow into little prigs (fearful of being contaminated by other people's values, and bristling with self-righteous indignation) instead of compassionate human beings. Yet if I open the door to the world, having taught them only to love all that lives, they will be broken by the storm of their desire to help in a nightmare of needs.

How to resolve this tension? Day by day, given grace. And, on the days when no grace seems available, by muddling through. Mostly it is a matter of emphasis, of trying to be sensitive to the rhythms of the child's growth. When our daughter Cricket was six, I realized that it was time—much as I loathed the idea of her entering the marketplace—for her to have an allowance. She didn't even know what an allowance was, nor had she expressed many desires for things which could be bought with an allowance, but soon enough she would be dazzled by the candy, gum, and playthings I dismissed as junk. I couldn't, wouldn't buy them for her, but she should weigh their value for herself. The allowance could be spent on anything, and—I specified—even on bubble gum and Barbie dolls, if they were her heart's desire.

Like the good little parent-pleaser she was, Cricket rarely spent her allowance on anything, although she delighted in having money to give away to people she loved. I was a little aghast at her desire-less-ness (having so generously "given" her autonomy!) until she began to challenge my taste for her in food, clothes, haircuts, etc. We had a painful few months until she helped me understand that the freedom to buy was nearly irrelevant: it was the freedom to be that she was starved for. Then I realized that, in all my meditating and decision-making, it was the that-of-God in me to whom I was turning. I did not trust that-of-God in her very much, except in the matter of the allowance! Time to get out of her way a bit...

In the spring, all the first-grade girls brought home Xeroxed invitations to join Bluebirds. Cricket handed me hers, with that opaque look which says, "Here's something you're probably not going to approve of." I asked her if she wanted to join. She did. Having been a Girl Scout myself, I had a flash of memory of high ideals stirred around in a stew of chocolate mint cookies, American flags, and busywork. But Cricket was seven years old, and second grade was the year of the Bluebird. I went to the organizational meeting of mothers, intending to hold my tongue. The mothers who had volunteered to lead the group were pleasant women with good intentions. The meetings could be held at school, to make it easy (and, since they viewed Bluebird meetings as weekly get-togethers over a cup of Kool-Aid and a cookie, it didn't matter that the school would not permit them the use of the gym, the kitchen, the art and music centers, or the storage space), but they did feel uniforms would be nice.

It is true that children love uniforms. The official red, white, and blue Bluebird uniform costs about $20. I suggested that a white shirt, blue jeans, and a red tie that the children could make themselves would identify the Bluebirds adequately, besides assuring that no child was likely to be excluded for financial reasons. No one else felt much enthusiasm for the makeshift alternative, but it would have been hard to reject such a practical solution. We agreed on shirts and blue jeans and ties.

Cricket looked forward eagerly to the first official Bluebirds meeting and came home sparkling with two bits of news: 1) Sears sells real Bluebird uniforms, with a dress and a cap and a pin, and lots of the girls already have theirs! Well, I said, the mothers had agreed on a different uniform; maybe she'd like to save her allowance to buy a cap or a pin. 2) The Bridge School Bluebirds are going to be in a parade in November! (A parade in November? What parade? In my heart of hearts, of course, I already knew: November 11—Armistice Day or Veterans' Day or whatever they are calling it these days. I had a flash of the head-on collision between my role as the mother of a marching Bluebird and my role as a war-tax resister, and I grappled for some time to think.) "Oh?" (I tried to be noncommittal.) "What's the parade about?" Cricket didn't know. I told her it was the responsibility of a good Bluebird and a good citizen to know what she was marching for. Some parades celebrate things she would want to celebrate, and some do not. I told her to ask her leader what the parade was for.

For several weeks, she conveniently "forgot" to ask this question. I fretted, stewed in my own juices, and searched for clarity in my journal. I could let the whole thing go—and she might never realize what was going on. But we couldn't tell her at the last minute that we weren't going to the parade because it was pro-war. How would she feel going off to march for something that her parents feel so strongly about they are willing to break the law rather than pay war taxes? Couldn't I just keep silent and go to the parade? No. Aside from my ego and the matter of my image in the community, she knew that her father and I had made the decision, after years of thought, to witness to the Peace Testimony. If we applauded this parade, sooner or later she would be confused and troubled by our inconsistency. It was important to support her, though, not to imply that she had made a bad choice in joining Bluebirds. She would have to decide for herself whether to march or not to march.

What a choice for a loving, loyal, seven-year-old: her parents' values or her friends'. I didn't even know what I hoped she'd choose! Maybe we could find a way out of this choice, but there would be a pack of similar dilemmas on its heels. I prayed for clearness: she was almost bound to choose to please us. The only clarity I could find was to trust her and insist that she accept the implications of her decision.

She came home from Bluebirds in mid-October and told me about the parade: "It's on November the 11th, and we're making a banner that says 'Bluebird Angels' because that's the name we picked, and I asked Mrs. Waibel and the parade is for the Weathermen." (The Weathermen! I had a flash of the Weather Underground emerging to march through Lexington Center on November 11 in the Bicentennial Year of 1976!) "The Weathermen?" "I think that's what she said." "...If it's November 11, I bet it's the Veterans..." "Yes, that's it! The Veterans!"

She didn't ask me who or what "the Veterans" were. I asked her if she knew. She didn't, and finally she asked. I took a deep breath: "Veterans are soldiers, who have fought in wars." "But I don't like soldiers!" We've been through this many times. "There's nothing wrong with soldiers, only with war. Soldiers are people just like everybody else. Your grandfather was a soldier. Even your daddy was a soldier, before he decided war was wrong. Many good people feel that even though war is terrible, sometimes you have to have a war. Everybody pays for the soldiers to fight. Some soldiers get killed. After the war, people feel they should thank the men who fought for them, and thank the families whose fathers or sons died fighting." "I don't want to be in the parade, if it's for war."

"You know that we feel war is wrong and you don't want to support war, but you do want to be with your friends in Bluebirds, don't you? You're only seven, and we don't expect you to believe everything we believe yet. It's okay if you want to do what the other Bluebirds do. It really is. You have to make up your own mind." "I want to be with my friends, but I don't want to be for war."

I was uncomfortable about constructing such a tight dilemma, but I felt there was truth in it. If you walk in a Veterans' Day parade, then you are implicitly supporting war as a solution to conflict. Cricket was near tears, and I ached for her. "Lots of people don't want war, but they don't say anything about being for peace. Everyone wants peace. Maybe you could march for peace." "YES!...but how could I?" "Maybe you could make a banner for peace." "What would I say?" "That's up to you. That's the hard part. If you're really for peace, it has to be because you believe in it yourself, not because we believe in it and you want to believe what we believe. You'll have to decide what you want to say about peace and you'll have to ask Mrs. Waibel." "But that's too hard." "Then you can march in the parade with your friends, or you can stay home. But if you decide to stay home, you'll have to tell your friends. You can't just not show up when they're counting on you. You'll have to explain." "Oh, NO!" There it was: either way, everyone will know that Cricket is a freak! "It's a very hard choice. Let me know whatever you decide, and I'll help you do whatever you want to do."

Two weeks went by. I didn't mention it, and neither did she. Then the phone rang. It was Gail Waibel, the Bluebird leader, sounding frantic. Cricket had told Heidi Waibel that the parade was for war, but she was for peace. Heidi said she was for peace, too. They decided they would carry a banner, and it would say: "Peace. No more wars. People need things." (I was thrilled. I had bent over backwards not to discuss any of the issues we had gone over at other times, but Cricket had gone straight to the essential connection between peace and social justice!)

Mrs. Waibel panicked, knowing full well that all the little girls would be against war, and imagined herself leading a troop of little protesters with peace signs down Massachusetts Avenue in the official Veterans' Day parade. I felt sorry for this nice, apolitical woman who had volunteered to make Kool-Aid and play games once a week. I told her I understood perfectly and that I had warned Cricket that it might not be possible to carry peace signs, since they would make some people very uncomfortable, that Cricket would have to choose between being in the parade as it was and staying home. "Oh, NO!" said Mrs. Waibel. "We don't want Cricket to stay home!"

Well, I observed that, after all, parades are for ideals. We had agonized over whether or not to burden Cricket with the ideal of peace but didn't feel ultimately that we had a choice, because, all around her, war was being idealized. In the Bicentennial Year, almost all attention in Lexington was being focused on battles. No one talks about the history of nonviolent revolution, even though there is some research being done. In fact, Gene Sharp, at Harvard, has suggested that the nonviolent resistance of the colonists had brought them to the edge of independence and the battles may actually have prolonged the process, etc., etc. (Mrs. Waibel was amazed: "That's fascinating! Why haven't I ever heard that before?") Cricket had decided she didn't want to march in a parade for war. Parades are about ideals, and her ideal was peace. How would Mrs. Waibel feel about a United Nations flag as a symbol of peace? We had one the Bluebirds could borrow. Of course, the UN was a feeble instrument of peace, but it was the best the world had for the moment.

Yes! Mrs. Waibel was all for peace and the UN, and Cricket could carry the flag. I said I didn't think Cricket cared about carrying the flag herself but that I was sure she'd feel glad to march if her group was carrying the UN flag. On the other hand, I went on, the UN was controversial in some circles, and even if Mrs. Waibel endorsed it, the other leader might not like the idea. It isn't that we don't want children to love the United States, but that we want them also to love the rest of the world. How about if the Bluebirds carried their banner, and an American flag, and a UN flag? Would that cover everything? Mrs. Waibel was pleased I had thought of all this and said she would check with her co-leader, but she was sure it would be fine. She called me the day before the parade. The Bluebird hierarchy had warned her about flag etiquette, and she had spent hours determining what size American flag was needed alongside our UN flag, on what height pole, and then locating the proper equipment.

That night Cricket was pale and tired, and looked like she was coming down with flu. In the morning, I tried to ignore all the symptoms of illness. The weather was wet and cold. In the middle of our hot breakfast, Cricket threw up. AAAARGH! After all this! I called Mrs. Waibel to tell her Cricket would not be marching, UN flag or not. Mrs. Waibel, predictably, was crushed. An hour before parade time, Cricket was looking and feeling fine, and we hoped she'd just had a twenty-four hour upset. We dressed her warmly and decided to take her and the flag to the starting point—and said that she could walk as far with her Bluebirds as she felt like walking.

Parade fever in the air: drums, jeeps, a skimpy unit of veterans and the ladies auxiliary. Mostly: Bluebirds, Campfire Girls, Brownies, Girl Scouts, Boy Scouts, and parents. Cricket hoisted the UN flag, Heidi the American flag, and the other Bluebirds stretched out the banner they had made. They walked the mile to the Green. No one noticed anything unusual—the single UN flag in a thicket of stars and stripes—but the Bluebirds knew. (Cricket had explained in her own words, and they thought it was fine.) Mrs. Waibel knew, too, and—when I thanked her for all her support—she said with graciousness and sincerity that she had learned something herself, and it had been a good experience for Heidi, too. Most of all, Cricket knew. She glowed.

At home, we thanked Cricket for the work she had done for peace. She shone with a new light—a sense of strength and purpose as well as love.

Epilogue

One week later, when Gail Waibel gave Cricket a ride home from Bluebirds, she leaned out the window apologetically, anticipating another ordeal, no doubt. "Once a year, all the Bluebirds sell candy to raise money. I don't like the idea, but all the troops have to do it." I winced. For years, the Bluebirds have rung my bell—and each year I've told them that I wouldn't buy candy but hoped they'd come back next year with nuts or raisins to sell. But this was no time to get into nutrition, good teeth, and world hunger. We can't react to every issue.

I could write to the Bluebirds, suggesting they support themselves and poor people at the same time by peddling Koinonia pecans. Meanwhile I could make it a small decision for Cricket. She loves pecans and would be happy to sell them next year, but this year she had 12 boxes of candy to sell. I'd be happy to buy one, and we could all eat it, but that's one more box sold, one less reason for the headquarters to switch to pecans. Cricket said no, not to buy one. I helped her figure out what neighbors to approach and what to say when they came to the door. She and her little brother set out on a high adventure—and, in less than an hour, were back, bright with success. She had sold 11 boxes of the 12. She herself purchased the last box—with one whole month's allowance! She offered candy to all, had a piece herself, and then it was over—the nearly-full box abandoned in the refrigerator.

I still haven't gotten around to writing the letter to Bluebird Headquarters. A few weeks ago, however, I gave Gail Waibel the *Fellowship* magazine with Gene Sharp's article on "Forgotten History," with a tactful note attached, telling her not to bother reading it if she wasn't interested. I'm not entirely comfortable with taking this initiative and have probably made her somewhat uncomfortable, too—but no one ever said peacework was easy.

"Let us take the risks of peace upon ourselves, not impose the risks of war upon the world." Not easily done, least of all when we are taking the risks of peace not only upon ourselves but upon our children. No laying trips on little children or Bluebird leaders—only loving initiatives grounded in prayer and openness to whatever response comes. We need to be very clear about the risks, humble about our efforts, and trustful of that-of-God in others as well as in ourselves. Teilhard de Chardin prayed it in these words: "Preserve in me a burning love for the world and a great gentleness...help me persevere to the end in the fullness of humanity."

March 2009

A Peace Education Sabbatical

by Susan Gelber Cannon

I believe in the culture of peace. I believe in daily peace-building on a personal, institutional, national, and international level. I believe in regular, not random, acts of kindness. I believe in the power of teachers and students to be peace-builders.

In March 2006, as a middle school teacher in an independent school outside Philadelphia, I was on sabbatical. Convinced that we everyday people are the key to creating a culture of peace in the world, I was preparing to travel halfway around the world to share my ideas on peace-building with teachers and students in Japan, China, Canada, and Denmark.

In many ways, this journey of thousands of miles started at home with my father, Fred. From my earliest memories, I can see images of my father in uniform. There were the tiny photographs (fading even in my childhood) that he shot in Italy in World War II. There he was holding up the Leaning Tower of Pisa, or posing with a buddy in a foxhole. In my memory, I can hear the stories, often funny, of how he and a buddy jumped waist-deep into a pigpen under orders to take cover, of getting stranded up a telephone pole when he was stringing wire as his jeep buddies sped away under German fire. My father told these stories over and over again, and they always ended with his loud belly laughs, as if he were trying to persuade us that the war had been fun.

But, I also hear the screaming. My father screamed in his sleep often, sometimes nightly, especially after watching a war movie. "Don't let him watch it," my mother would plead. "He'll fight the war all night if he does." But my dad always wanted to watch; it was as if he had to. He paid for each viewing with refreshed images in his nightmares. He would awaken my mom as he kicked and twitched, flailed and yelled, working the covers off his bruised and purple legs, battle-scarred and discolored from freezing in the Italian Alps in the winter of 1944.

My father had written my mother every day during the war, and we have over 1,000 letters he sent her, full of love, loneliness, and longing, but missing any mention of war's horrors. He never talked seriously about the war until he was in his 80s, when my sixth-grade son conducted a video interview for a school project. Again, my dad told the funny stories, but suddenly, after two hours, he got serious, calling for his Army-issue Bible, a battered leather-covered copy that he had kept in his pocket every day of the war. He read the 23rd Psalm aloud. "'The Lord is my Shepherd; I shall not want.' I read that verse every day in battle," my father confided, looking straight at the camera, telling the truth even though he knew we could not fully understand it:

War is hell. That first battle was my baptism by fire. I was one of the walking wounded. . . . Those times weren't a vacation and it wasn't a game. There were thousands of dead people lying around—not just one—but thousands. . . . There were dead soldiers everywhere. . . . War is hell. I don't wish it on my best friends or my worst enemy. May my children, and my grandchildren and my great-grandchildren be spared from it, forever. Amen.

"Okay," my father concluded. "Now you can shut off the camera." Unfortunately, we couldn't shut off the war in his mind.

The Secret World of War

The combat veteran lives in a world apart. The civilian co-worker, friend, wife, husband, child, parent—knows nothing about this world. Aware of our ignorance, countless poets and writers have tried to translate the soldier's and veteran's inner life to the rest of us. As I went searching for peace-builders during my sabbatical year, I encountered two of them early in the process, at Wilmington College's Westheimer Peace Symposium. Contemporary war correspondent Chris Hedges writes compellingly about war's horrors in two books, *War is a Force that Gives Us Meaning*, and *What Every Person Should Know About War*. His work does much to help ordinary citizens like me understand the realities—not the myth—of war. Here is an excerpt from a newspaper commentary by him, "The Myth and Reality of War" (*Philadelphia Inquirer*, Sept. 18, 2005):

War, it must be recognized, even for those who support the conflict . . . distorts and damages those sent to fight it. No one walks away from prolonged exposure to such violence unscathed, although not all come back disturbed. Our leaders mask the reality of war with abstract words of honor, duty, glory, and the ultimate sacrifice. These words, obscene and empty in the midst of combat, hide the fact that war is venal, brutal, disgusting.

John Crawford, an Iraq War veteran, was a senior in college when his Army Reserves unit was sent to Iraq. An accidental soldier, he published his war writing in his book *The Last True Story I'll Ever Tell*. Reading it and talking with John, I understood more clearly the transformation from student to soldier he had undergone. "They wanted me to act like a man, but I was feeling like a little boy," he said. "I never wanted to hate anyone; it just sort of happens that way in a war."

After my father's death, I asked my 90-year-old mother, "How did Dad go through all he did and still carry on a normal life?" "He fought the war every night," she replied, and turned away. He wasn't alone. Millions of veterans of combat, soldier and civilian alike, are still living with the demons of war both in their daily lives and in their nightmares. And every day, in numerous countries around the world, more men, women, and children are becoming living and dead casualties of war, military and civilian alike.

As a daughter, a sister, a wife, a mother, and a teacher, I want to know why we are allowing this as a global society. I have not raised my two sons to kill other mothers' sons. I am not teaching my students so they can go out and kill the students of other teachers. In my classroom, I refuse to support the myth of war anymore. I want to create a culture of peace.

Learnings from a Sabbatical

A sabbatical is an opportunity for a teacher to do research in a field of interest, away from the demands of the classroom. For my sabbatical during the school year 2005–06, I researched, wrote, created the website <www.teachforpeace.org>, and taught and traveled overseas. My field of interest was and continues to be peace education.

Peace education aims to change an existing belief system—acceptance of war as a method of solving international problems—to a new paradigm—one in which human rights, social justice, sustainable development, and creative diplomacy are promoted as effective paths to national and international security. Peace education helps young people see themselves as integral parts of one human family and as capable actors for positive social change on a local and global stage. In short, peace education helps kids to think, care, and act.

I traveled all around the world looking for peace educators and peace-builders. Upon my return, it was important for me to share my thoughts and experiences with the middle and upper school students at my school. Many were inspired, referring to my ideas in later talks of their own. Here are some of the things I told them:

• I learned that the modern, built-up city of Hiroshima, Japan, with its parks, shops, and skyscrapers, still has the eerie feeling of the dead, those who were incinerated by the atomic bomb. But life goes on. People work, shop, and picnic; children play and laugh.

• I learned that hibakushas, A-bomb survivors, speak every day to groups of school children from middle schools all over Japan, about the perils of nuclear weapons and the horrors of war.

• I learned from one hibakusha, Michiko Yamoake-san, that she would keep speaking to group after group of children even though she was ill, reasoning, "If I speak to 100 children, and I reach just one . . . that one might make a difference."

• I learned that if I also speak up, and if even one student feels moved, that is a good thing.

• I learned from college students in Kyoto that Japanese students feel pressured throughout their school careers, having to take exam after exam, and worrying about getting into college, just like my U.S. students.

• And I learned that once they get there, they feel worried about getting jobs and good houses, and have no time to worry about issues such as equality and peace.

• From these students, and others in China, I learned that it is important to teach my students how to balance their lives so they can think about important issues, while doing the things they need to do to succeed personally.

• I learned in Toyohashi, Japan, that private school students in Sakara-goake Middle School could choose a global education track that would enable them to travel and learn about countries around the world for the next five years of their schooling. This was their school's answer to the horrors of Japanese military aggression during World War II.

• I learned that in Japan, once the home of innovative peace education, nationalism is on the rise. Teachers who buck countrywide proposals to teach "patriotism" in Japanese schools find their job security threatened.

Teachers who refuse to rise for the singing of the national anthem, for example, have been fined, suspended, or sent by their school districts to distant schools as Japan begins to remilitarize.

• Knowing how quickly patriotism turns to nationalism and then to militarism makes many educators—like me—apprehensive. I determined that I would teach teachers in the United States, and other countries I visit, about ways to teach for peace and an inclusive commitment to local, national, and global citizenship during our daily lessons, even at the risk of losing popularity or job security.

• I learned in Toyohashi, Japan, that artists and educators can work together on peace projects, even when they cannot understand each others' languages, to create beautiful works of art for peace.

• I learned how inspiring the work of a small group can be to others. One Japanese artist wrote, "You taught us how to express our own opinion. You gave me energy. We have to start some action like you. The Toyohashi Peace Event was a great lesson for us."

• I learned in Xinglong County, China, how comforting it feels to be treated to wonderful food and caring guidance in a new country, and that hospitality is a gracious talent at which my Chinese hosts were masters. I vowed to be a better host when people visit my home, my school, and my country.

• I learned in Xinglong County, in Beijing, Shanghai, and countless cities in China, how curious many Chinese people are about people in the United States, and that they will open their homes and schools to meet these visitors and make new friends.

• I learned that Chinese middle school students can be just as energetic, noisy, fun, smart, kind, and naughty as my U.S. middle school students, and I felt at home teaching them.

• I learned how important it is for people in the United States to learn about Chinese culture, history, and development, and that the future of the world may well be found in the quality of the relationships among these two peoples. I made a website to help U.S. students learn about life in China, and another one to help Chinese learn about life in the United States. Many of my students are pictured on the website, and teachers and students all over the world have enjoyed their writing and artwork about their hopes and dreams.

• I also learned that many people who used to look at the United States with admiration now look at us with fear. "What is going on with your country?" was the most common question we were asked in Japan, China, Denmark, and Canada. However, another comment we heard quite often was, "We thought all Americans were arrogant and selfish—until we met you." I realized the power of personal connection in a global society.

• I learned from one Japanese woman that her post office was powered by solar panels on the roof. In Yangzhou and Rugao, China, I saw passive solar water heaters on every rooftop. I learned from my Danish hosts about water-conserving toilets. "Why can't you Americans do things like this?" they asked. We can. Our new toilet works beautifully and saves water.

• I learned that my Chinese teacher friends walk, ride bikes, or take long bus rides to get to their schools each day, yet I know they wish they could drive to work as I usually do. I saw Chinese cities developing at a seemingly unsustainable pace and wondered how our two countries will solve problems of pollution and competition for resources in a sustainable manner. The point is: We must.

• I learned in Canada, at an international conference of peace researchers, that all over the world, in any country I could name, people are working on projects big and small to promote peace.

• I learned from Johan Galtung, Norwegian peace mediator, that many citizens of the world want Americans to walk humbly, to realize that we are a nation among nations, and that we need to cooperate with the world community.

• I learned in Denmark that in a climate of distrust, reasoned, responsible free speech can promote dialogue and understanding, while flippant, irresponsible free speech can destroy dialogue. I learned that ignorance of the culture of your neighbor can lead to violence with your neighbor.

• I learned in Norway, at the Nobel Institute, that everyone can be a peacebuilder. I interviewed Anne Kjelling, chief librarian, and asked her what my students most needed to know. "Tell them anyone can be a Nobel Peace Prize winner. They are just ordinary people, educated and uneducated, doctors, lawyers, housewives, volunteers. The thing is, they have done something for the cause of peace. Everyone can, but no one does," she said. I vowed that I would tell my U.S. students that.

• I learned from Irwin Abrams, Nobel Peace Prize biographer, U.S. historian, peace educator, and Quaker, that peace education leads to an "unseen harvest." He was emphatic. "There are consequences" of the peace work we do. Big and small efforts yield fruit, whether we are the ones to harvest it or not. He encouraged me to believe that my efforts as a teacher are meaningful and important, even in a culture of war.

• Finally, I learned that in Danish, Swedish, and Norwegian, Fred means Peace. I was visiting the Nobel Fredcenter when I figured it out.

Being an Active Peace-builder

My father's name was Fred. While he didn't have peace in his life, his name, his experiences, and his love for people propel me to work for Fred, for Paz, Heiwa, He Ping, Salaam, Shalom, Shanti, Peace.

I want my students to believe in the value of active peace-building: the belief that socially just policies and structures are more lastingly effective methods of solving global problems than violence and war. Finally, I want them to know that such pacifism is not passive. It is active, hard work, and it is not for the faint of heart.

I ask that my students be peace-builders, encouraging them by saying, "Use your critical judgment when you watch TV or read the news. Walk, take the bus, carpool. Buy less stuff. Be a good host. Do regular acts of kindness. Study about other cultures, religions, and countries. Make friends with people who are different from you. Care about your families and classmates, and also care about the billions of people who are your global neighbors. Learn how to select a cause worthy of your energy and work for it. Make time for peace-building. Think. Care. Act. 'Everyone can, but no one does.' Be the one who does."

August 1997

Bringing Nonviolence Workshops
to School

by Fenna Mandolang

Nonviolence is highly valued in my family, and I love new experiences, so I decided to bring a series of three, three-day nonviolence workshops to my middle school. My mother spoke to the principal, and they wrote a grant proposal to purchase manuals and supplies. The principal said if students liked the workshops, they would continue; if not, they would stop. So I made a decision to make a difference and try to keep the program alive. I didn't know what I was getting into, but I did know the first step was to become a facilitator.

I had to complete three, three-day workshops: basic, advanced, and training for facilitators. I also tried to encourage other participants by practicing what we were taught and by talking to them outside the workshops. I wanted as many different kinds of kids as possible to enjoy the workshops; this wasn't too hard because the program captured them by itself. Each workshop requires a team of three to five volunteer facilitators. It is important to have a student perspective on the facilitation team, but it's hard to get volunteers to facilitate. Many people want to take the workshop, but we are very low on serious facilitators. The other thing I had to do that was vital to keeping the workshops was to speak with the teachers and support the school sponsor of the project. My mother and I talked to the teachers at a faculty and staff meeting. She talked about the history of the workshops and their importance to her. I talked about why I thought they were important for the students and the school and how I benefited from them. I am still facilitating workshops and learning new things every time.

Help Increase the Peace Project (HIPP) is a series of nonviolence workshops for up to 25 kids in middle or high school. At Belle Vue Middle School, we have offered four basic, one advanced, and one training for facilitators since September 1994. We have trained 16 facilitators, eight of whom are active. The workshops are open to all kinds of students: leaders, troublemakers, and average kids. A few adults from the school or community are allowed to participate. The workshops are hands-on activities and voluntary for all participants and facilitators. One-hour mini-workshops after school give a refresher to anyone who's been through a workshop and provide apprenticing opportunities.

In the workshops, we learn skills that help prevent fights and create a friendly, fun atmosphere. These skills include good communication, affirmation, cooperation, and transforming power. All of these skills are important for many different reasons. Learning about good communication is valuable because you can stop a fight before it starts by eliminating assumptions and making sure you go to the source of the negativity and clearly state your message without being rude or disrespectful. Affirmation is essential because you have to have good self-esteem to do most things well. HIPP emphasizes being positive and that it's okay to say good things about yourself and others. Cooperation is important because if you are not willing to cooperate and at least listen to the other side, you will have a rough time coming to a win/win situation (where everyone is satisfied). Most kids have at least heard of these skills, but many kids don't have a lot of practice, and most have never heard of transforming power.

Transforming power is the opposite of the power of violence. When someone is annoying or violent, it's so easy to get mad at them. That's the power of violence. Transforming power is the power to change a situation so that it becomes a manageable, or maybe even a constructive, situation. It is the power of truth, the power of caring, the power of respect. Transforming power means you have to be open to all kinds of solutions: surprise, humor, patience, persistence, or being serious. Using transforming power is hard because it isn't letting people take advantage of you. It requires strength, courage, self-respect, and respect for others. It isn't safer than violence; it involves taking risks. It's just a choice between different kinds of risks. All of this information is usually new to participants, so we go around giving examples of when we have used or seen transforming power.

All of these skills are very useful and very helpful, but they wouldn't have the impact if it weren't for the community we build among the people. The community building starts from the minute we begin until the minute we end and still carries on afterward. Everyone has an image at school, but we try to mix with everyone and treat everyone with respect. Everyone—no matter old or young, rich or poor, participant or facilitator—is equal. Facilitators introduce and state rules of activities, but we also always participate. Another reason we form community is because we build trust. One of the ground rules is to observe confidentiality. It is hard to describe the trust that is formed. People open up and share things you would never have expected. You have to actually interact with the kids that seem so different to find out we aren't so different after all and learn to appreciate the differences between people.

The experience is what captures me every time. Every time it is different. Every time I hear a new set of sad and happy stories. I meet new people with different cultures, families, and varieties of experiences. I become good friends with someone no one would have ever expected. It reminds me to be thankful for what I have and opens my eyes to a whole new world. This is just the way it affects me. Everyone gains something different. Some people come out with a new understanding of nonviolence, and whether they practice what they have learned or not is up to them, but at least they are aware of it. Other participants come out with better skills and know what they might do to help prevent violence. There are other participants who come out with their lives changed completely.

I know a guy whose family is very prejudiced. In the basic workshop, he talked about his experience and found a new confidence about himself and his views. He knew he couldn't change his family, but he could change himself. He was the one who stopped Checker Day last year. Checker Day is when a rumor goes around that on a certain day, whites and blacks will jump each other and fight for no reason. When the rumor came to him, he said he wasn't going to be involved, so his friends said they wouldn't be involved. Some of the black kids who knew him from HIPP asked him what was going to happen on Checker Day, and he said that nothing was going to happen. The teachers and administrators heard and were afraid, but nothing happened last year. I can walk around the school now and say hi to all kinds of kids I would have never known and been afraid of before. They say hi, and we watch out for each other, even though we're really different. That makes the school feel different.

I will continue to facilitate workshops. We have three more planned. Then we'll have a new group of facilitators and make new plans with them. I will continue to work on my facilitation skills. I'm confident with the simple activities and have begun to work on giving instructions or introductions to the more complicated or critical activities. I hope to be a lead facilitator soon, to give others the opportunity to apprentice and develop confidence in their skills.

We have had requests to share our work from around Florida and Georgia. Two U.S. youth trainers went to Miami to present our project to people who wanted to know about it there. Responding to these requests, we're trying to schedule a training series in Orlando. I've arranged for group rates for participants to take the train, the Friends meetinghouse offered a meeting room and overnight cottage, and I've made shopping and cooking lists. It takes a great deal of time, but I think it's worth it!

December 1, 1962

Counseling Young Friends on the Draft

by Lawrence Lee

It says much for George Fox's faith and example that Friends meetings have uniformly supported the Peace Testimony, although they vary in degree of active participation. But, regrettably, these same meetings have been apathetic toward the question of military service. It is, nonetheless, their duty to provide guidance on this subject.

In order to decide whether or not to accept combatant service, the young Friend who is drafted must have a sound grounding in spiritual life and civic responsibility, together with a familiarity with all the alternatives to combatant service, the problems involved, and the consequences of his decision. He must be able to count on his meeting's willingness to recognize and explore the issues and possible solutions, as well as to welcome and accept responsibility for the individual member's actions. There should be a prevailing sense of meeting support and acquiescence in the young Friend's eventual decision and an open, unembarrassed attitude toward the question.

Whatever decision ultimately is made, the young Friend's peace of mind and satisfaction will depend directly upon the amount of meeting support and backing given to him. He must feel a common purpose and understanding.

The meeting, to fulfill its duties, must adopt a positive plan of education, discussion, and formal counseling. The following are suggested as a minimum to achieve the necessary atmosphere:

• Begin advising and counseling parents in their responsibilities to their sons on this aspect of the Peace Testimony before the boys reach draft age.

• Arrange lectures, classes, and conferences dealing with responsibility to conscience and country for pre-teenagers and all young Friends up to draft age.

• Counsel both the young Friend and his parents on the requirements of the draft, the available alternatives, and the consequences of his decision.

• Render individual and private counseling to the young Friend on the meeting's concept of the Peace Testimony.

• Make available to him information about such counseling agencies as the Central Committee for Conscientious Objectors, the National Service Board for Religious Objectors, and the American Friends Service Committee.

• Devote time in monthly meetings or other group gatherings to discussion on the meeting's attitude toward the Peace Testimony and military service.

• Insure that the Peace Committee or other responsible individuals are available to any Friend for open discussion of the issue.

• Instruct the young Friend on the history and traditions of Friends in action for peace.

If the meeting seizes the initiative, treats this service issue as a significant concern, and devotes its energies to the question on a continuing basis, it will impart to each young Friend facing this decision the necessary knowledge and strength to make his choice. Having made it, he will be able to bear with it for life in the peace of mind, security, and well-being that a "loving" meeting should give him.

April 2008

You, Too, Can Rein in Military Recruiters in the High School

by Nancy Howell and Judy Alves

In the spring of 2005, military recruiters had free rein in some of the high schools of Lee County, Florida (which includes Fort Myers, Cape Coral, and surrounding communities, with almost 80,000 students in our public schools). Military recruiters from the Army, Marines, Navy, and Air Force set up tables and exercise equipment in the lunchrooms, courtyards, and hallways of schools, giving away tokens of military life and signing up students for more information, for special exercise and computer games based on military life, and for free trips to the nearest military enlistment center in Tampa. Many of the schools assigned a day a week to each branch of the military for recruiting, and all the schools turned over home addresses and phone numbers of students to the military so that they could contact them at their leisure.

By coincidence, we had both retired from demanding jobs and moved to the Fort Myers area a year or so before we started working against recruiting in high schools. Nancy had recently retired as a professor of Sociology from University of Toronto, and Judy retired from the practice of law. With our own children grown up, an interest in youth, and frustration over the occupation of Iraq, we both felt called to the work of counter-recruitment.

Our starting point was a great weekend workshop put on by Oskar Castro of American Friends Service Committee in Philadelphia. Nancy had heard him speak at the 2005 Southeastern Yearly Meeting in Leesburg, Florida. On invitation, Oskar came to Fort Myers Meeting a few months later to work with a group of 12 members of the meeting, plus seven local peace activists who wanted to hear what he had to say. Oskar pointed out that it is easier to work in the public schools as a secular group than as a project of a religious society, and Fort Myers Meeting, where Nancy is a member, agreed to support our efforts but not sponsor them.

We did not want to get bogged down in organizational issues; "Just do it" has always been our motto. So we selected a name, "The Wage Peace Project"; had some business cards printed up; and set out to learn about how military recruiting is organized locally and what we could do to apply what Oskar had taught us about counter-recruiting. We share the title "co-chair," and we have no other officers or committees. We personally have done 90 percent of the work of the project, with help at busy times from an informal circle of a dozen or so people willing to pitch in when needed. We called it a "project" as an acknowledgment of what our neighbors in Palm Beach, Florida, had done with their counter-recruiting group, "The Truth Project." And we borrowed "wage peace" from AFSC, in large part because we guessed that high school students would like to have those popular rubber bracelets with Wage Peace printed on them that AFSC distributes.

We thought it would be useful to have 501(C)(3) status, so we applied to our local group, the Environmental and Peace Education Center, led by Friend Phyllis Stanley and Bobbie Heinrich, to be adopted as its project. The board of directors of EPEC accepted our proposal without wishing to exercise tight control over our activities. They could not provide funding for us, but we figured we would have tax-exempt status later if we needed to do fundraising. (In fact, we haven't had to do any as we followed a strategy of keeping our expenses low and paying them ourselves.) We rented a mailbox from the local UPS store, to avoid using our home addresses.

We started by attending the Lee County School Board meetings as observers, and within a month we wrote to the superintendent of schools to inform him that we were organized as an official counter-recruiting group and that we intended to exercise our court-given rights to have the same access to students as the schools give to the military recruiters (*see sidebar, p.33*).

The superintendent of schools delegated the issue of counter-recruiting to the official school district attorney, who studied the question for some weeks and then met with us. We were informed that each school had its own policy set by its principal. When we made appointments to talk with the individual principals, we found that they were all unwilling to discuss their policy in detail without guidance from the school district attorney, and in fact we received a series of identically worded letters from principals, suggesting that they were all guided by the attorney on their responses. Eventually, the school board attorney met with us and acknowledged what we already knew: that the federal circuit courts had given permission for counter-recruiters to go into the schools, to have equal access with the military, and to present the negative side of military enlistment to the students. After he informed the principals of his conclusion, the doors opened. We tried to be as non-confrontational as we could be, and we agreed to submit our proposed literature to the attorney's office for review before submitting it to the principals of schools.

We started with an AFSC brochure, *Ten Points to Consider Before You Sign an Enlistment Agreement*, and we had to argue point by point and word by word with the school board attorney. Eventually, however, he "passed" the modified document and allowed us to append a sentence saying, "This pamphlet has been modified from one produced by the American Friends Service Committee. It has been reviewed and determined to be legally permissible by the Lee County School Board attorney for distribution in the high schools of Lee County." With this clearance, the principals felt confident in allowing us to put the pamphlet in their career counseling centers, to be distributed next to the military recruiting literature.

By the time we got our first pamphlet approved, the school year of 2005–2006 was almost over. We met with each of the career counselors at the 11 large high schools to let them know what we planned for the next school year. It was clear that they would cooperate with us as far as the principals authorized them to do so, and no further. In five schools, we would match the military recruiters by setting up a table in the courtyard or lunchroom and actively counter-recruit over lunchtime one day each week. In four schools where the military recruiters were restricted to the career counselor's office, we would merely phone each week and only go when a student requested an appointment with us. And in two schools we could only display literature in the career counselor's office, because the military recruiters were not allowed to actively recruit in those schools.

The routine during the 2006–2007 school year was to go to a school around 10:30 A.M. and set up a table and a display board with a heading like "The military is not just a job—it is eight years of your life."

When the first lunch bell rang, students poured out of classrooms headed for some calories, and we offered a leaflet to the curious on their way. Usually, serious conversations would not start until after they had eaten; then they would gather around our table, some friendly, many curious, and a few belligerent. Students told us about their fears for their brothers and sisters in the military; their concerns about the plans of their boyfriends and girlfriends; and their own plans for the future, in the military or outside of it. Some told us that they were already in the military, by which they meant that they had signed a Delayed Entry Program (DEP) contract, promising to go to Basic Training as soon as they graduated. And others told us about fighting off a steady barrage of phone calls and letters from recruiters in the various branches of the military, even though they had no interest in joining. Some of those who seemed to be headed for enlistment appeared to be very mature and knowledgeable about military careers, while others seemed to have little information and understanding. Some were very interested in what we had to say, while others were unwilling to hear us express concerns about the dangers and difficulties of military life for young people.

We provided information about pay, the terms of enlistment, and the problems with the Montgomery G.I. Bill of Rights. We handed out a range of pamphlets over the school year, such as *Ask a Recruiter; You Don't Have to Join the Military to Go to College*; and *Help Wanted*, on jobs locally available. Our single most powerful piece of literature, one that we always try to have at our counter-recruiting table, is a blank copy of the enlistment document, so that we can point out to students exactly where it says in the Department of Defense enlistment form that any promises made to them (including promises made by recruiters) that are not explicitly written in this contract are invalid and will not be honored; that the length of the term of enlistment is eight years; and that the government is entitled to change all the conditions of the contract at any time, while the recruit is committed to every aspect of the contract, under penalty of law and prison.

Our task for the summer of 2006 was trying to raise consciousness of the right of parents to opt out of allowing the schools to turn over home information about their child to the military for recruitment purposes. Only 25 percent of the parents had located this box and checked it during the 2005 school year (before we started). We carried out a campaign by leafleting local fairs, and by writing letters to the editors and guest opinion pieces in our local papers, which resulted in a rate of opt-out of 46 percent in 2006, an encouraging increase. During that school year we urged the school district to revise the form so that parents would find it easier to read and understand. They agreed, and improved it greatly, and in 2007 the percentage of parents who opted out in the 11 large schools was 55 percent, a clear majority. We urged the school board to interpret that as a vote by parents to restrict the recruiters in the schools, too.

We tried various strategies, mimicking the military recruiters. We gave away candy, cheap pins, and rubber bracelets. All the giveaways were popular with students. We experimented with showing counter-recruiting films in the public libraries after school, but found that virtually no students came to see them (although we met some nice adults who wandered in). We invested work and stamps to send a mailing to parents in a high recruitment area where we could not meet students in the lunchrooms (because the school had a policy of only allowing recruiting in the career counselor's office, by appointment), but we got no answers or signs of interest from parents. Live and learn. However, some of our efforts were unexpectedly successful. We put together a website and handed out pencils with the web address printed on them, and got more than 100,000 hits in the month of December 2006.

Did we change anyone's mind about enlistment? We know that at our 11 large schools, of less than 3,000 graduating seniors, 55 announced that they were going directly into the military in 2006, whereas 45 made the same statement in 2007. However, we hesitate to claim success in reducing enlistments since during the time we were raising consciousness about this issue, the war became increasingly unpopular and fewer people supported the President's plan for the surge of troops and the increased numbers of military abroad. We know only that we talked with thousands of students, parents, and others about the truth of military enlistment.

Throughout the 2006–2007 school year we regularly attended school board meetings, and we often took the opportunity of the three-minute public commentary period to remind the board and the community of our interest in this issue, and what we were learning. At the end of the school year, Nancy spoke about the varying policies in the 11 large high schools, and a school board member questioned the difference in the policies and asked the superintendent to look into it. At a meeting of high school principals with the superintendent in July 2007, the decision was made to standardize the policy for all the schools. From now on, military recruiters are restricted to recruiting only in the guidance or career counseling office, and only when a student requests an interview with a specific recruiter. Our counter-recruiting literature will continue to be displayed and available to students.

We are very pleased with this result. It means that students in the middle schools and in the early years of high school will not encounter military recruiters on school grounds, and that the older students will only encounter them at their own request. We are encouraged to find that our efforts were rewarded by attention and consideration from the school district officials and the community.

Why did we succeed in a relatively short period of time? The law was basically on our side, and the school authorities were committed to following the law and respecting the parents' wishes when they could do so. No doubt the fact that one of our co-chairs is a lawyer with no fear of having to go to court to get the benefits promised in law added greatly to our persuasiveness. We also made it easier for them by being non-confrontational, by agreeing that it would be inappropriate for us to engage in criticism of the President and his policies with students on school property. We expressed our respect for veterans and troops whenever we could, and often mentioned that the JROTC program is not a target of our work, as they are engaged in leadership training and education about the military, not recruitment. In the 2007–08 school year, the military has reduced its activities in the schools of Lee County. They phone the students who have not opted out, and try to get them to request appointments in the Career Counseling office, but the volume of such appointments has gone down. The Marine Corps attempted to recruit teachers and counselors to help them influence students, and offered to pay for trips to Parris Island and for catered lunches for teachers, but when we asked the school board attorney about such gifts, a message went out to all principals and counselors that the practice must be stopped.

Of course, we haven't solved the problem. The war goes on, young people go on killing and dying, and the brutality of the war continues to harm their bodies, minds, and spirits. We would like to do more, but the Spirit urges us to do what we can, and to share the results of our efforts with others. We want to help when possible with the similar struggles going on in other communities. We are sure there are many communities where young people would benefit if the military recruiters could be restrained to the limits of the law.

(Sidebar)
The Legal Bases of Recruiting and Counter-recruiting in High Schools

All 18-year-old young men (not women) must voluntarily register for the draft using a form (SSS Form 1M (UPO)) available at post offices and on the Internet, despite the absence of a draft since 1973. Failure to register disqualifies young men from government jobs and university funds and loans. There is no opening to claim conscientious objector status on the Selective Service registration form so COs must keep a file documenting their objection to war in their own papers. Dated documentation of discussions of war between the young person and either clergy or a clearness committee is usually the best way to establish CO status. COs do not have to be members of Peace Churches, but it helps to establish the legitimacy of the claim.

Schools must follow the No Child Left Behind Act: Section 85, which states that schools must give the military services access to students for recruiting purposes equal to that provided to recruiters from universities, colleges, and employers. Military recruiters often have far more access to students than required by law.

This law requires school boards to turn over directory information on students in high schools—including name, address, phone, school subjects, e-mail addresses, and other personal information—to each branch of the military service that requests it, for contact at home outside of school hours. Parents and students are permitted by NCLB to opt out by signing a form available at the beginning of the school year to deny access to directory information for that student.

Counter-recruiters are permitted in the public schools as a result of a series of court cases. Military recruiting has been found by judges to be a controversial issue in high schools, so the rights of those presenting the other side to be heard are protected. The main cases are:

- Clergy and Laity Concerned v. Chicago Board of Education (586 F. Supp. 1408, 1984)
- Searcy v. Harris (888 F. 2d 1314, 11th Circuit 1989)
- San Diego CARD v. Grossmont Union High School District (790 F.2d 1471, 9th Circuit 1986)
- Boucher v. School Board of Greenfield (134 F.3rd 821, 7th Circuit, 1998)
- Shanley v. NE Indiana School District (462 F.2d 960, 1972)
- Atlanta Federal Appellate Case Guarantees Equal Access to Schools for Military Critics (815 F.2d 1389 38 Ed.Law Rep.929, cite as 815 F.2d 1389)
- Emory Searcey, et. Al, Plaintiffs–Appellee v. Alonzo Crim, et. Al, Defendants-Appellants, United States of America, Intervenor-Defendant, Appellee, No. 86-8681. US Court of Appeals, Eleventh Circuit, April 17, 1987
- San Diego Federal Appellate case Guarantees Equal Access to Schools for Military Critics (790 F.2d 1471, 55 USLW 2007, 32 Ed.Law Rep. 467, 12 Media L. Rep. 2329 (cite as 790 F.2d 1471) submitted March 11, 1985, decided June 6,1986

August 2000

ROTC Revisited

by Katherine van Wormer

In June 1994 FRIENDS JOURNAL published my article "Challenging a Creeping Military Presence." The subject was ROTC. Among the guidelines offered in it was this: "Be prepared for a huge backlash when the arguments are made public. There will be a barrage of letters to the editor," etc.

This was written, of course, before the Internet and email revolution turned the communications process upside down, and before the U.S. Congress quashed virtually all opposition to military science by passing legislation to withdraw federal funding from universities that refused to house ROTC on their campuses. The funding to be withdrawn involved not only Defense Department contracts, but all financial aid for students.

Fast-forward to September 1999: *U.S. News and World Report* published its annual edition of "Best Colleges in the United States." A subsequent issue devoted to financial aid played up the ROTC scholarship in the most glowing terms. In reaction to this biased report, I fired off the following angry letter to the editor of *U.S. News and World Report*, October 4, 1999:

> How disturbed I was to see your article in the September 6 issue about ROTC scholarships as a means of providing funds for a college education. The education associated with ROTC is a contradiction to the academic freedom enjoyed at university campuses; military training on college campuses, in fact, makes a mockery of education. Far from taking a global view of learning, ROTC encourages narrow patriotism and a philosophy of any means (killing people and polluting environments) to the end. The institutionalized mistreatment of gays and lesbians in the military and sexual harassment of women are par for the course.

Before I had even seen the published letter, irate phone calls were coming in from bewildered yet outraged callers from all branches of the military.

The first week I received around 50 email letters, ordinary letters, and phone calls. On the seventh day, the letters dwindled to two. After answering the most sincere and thoughtful letters, I resumed my usual routines.

Then on Monday of the following week, I arrived at work to find 77 email messages on the screen. The next day over 100; then over 150. Among the subject headings were:

Do you know Jane Fonda? Shame on you!

Ignorant Professor

Traitor

ROTC

Did you write this? Commie bitch

No sooner had I read one message than another would pop up on the screen. Most of the letters were lengthy and addressed to long lists of military personnel in addition to selected administrators and colleagues at my university. Typically, correspondents forwarded my original letter from *U.S. News and World Report*, which now contained a lengthy rebuttal by an army captain. Many of the writers urged the readers to "write her and tell her what you think of her views on the military." One letter added: "Warning: she is a pacifist."

All this attention is a reflection of the revolution in communication, a revolution that can inform hundreds or thousands of people instantaneously of a happening and forward messages everywhere all at once. In this case, specialized Internet news groups such as <www.sci.military .naval>, <www.soe.veterans>, <www.alt.military>, and <www.FreeRepublic .com> presented my letter with various unquakerly replies. As one writer confirmed, "By now your email address is all over every military establishment this side of heaven itself." "I hope all these emails jam up your computer," said another.

Over 2,000 emails later (the peak in one day was over 150) I can now analyze some of the basic themes. First, what stands out is the rage: venom poured forth in message after message from those who live a harsh life toward one who clearly does not. For example: I am called a "menace to the young"; "a disgrace to an already disgraceful profession (social work)"; "a radical feminist"; "a lesbian who belongs on an island with others of her kind"; "a comrade of Hanoi Jane"; "a holdover from the 60s—were you a flower child?"

Sample comments sent to my university dean and president are: "I can't believe you allow a socialist to teach at your university." "Send her packing." "In case you are unaware of what the professor is up to, here is a copy of her letter."

Sarcasm was frequent, as in "I can't wait to get back to work harassing women and polluting the environment." As were disclaimers: "We are the true social workers." "We endure incredible hardships so that you can voice your idiotic opinions."

Whereas the military officers often spoke of me in the third person to their friends, army wives and parents of servicemen and -women tended to be more direct. Instructions to me were to: "Get your head out of the sand!" "Resign at once and take the first plane to some communist country." "Come down from your ivory tower and see the real world." "Join up or shut up." "Fall down on your hands and knees and thank the men and women in the military for the freedoms you seem so willing to abuse."

Looking back over these reams of angry accusation, re-reading them or really reading them, I am able to get a sense of something that goes beyond the bravado, name-calling, and stilted military rhetoric. I am able to grasp their suffering and even feel from their point of view, their bitterness against an unexpected outside attack, an attack by a civilian no less, and one who enjoys a life of relative ease. What does it mean, I wonder, to live a regimented life in isolation from family and friends? And to be at the constant beck and call of barking officials in uniform?

No longer can I disregard their stories, stories of risky missions and heroism and grief. Many such personal narratives are punctuated by pleas of "Don't delete"; or "Hear my story." Getting beyond the insults, then, I do hear their stories and in so doing enter a different landscape, far from the sanctuary of my academic office. I learn, for example, of the disabled veteran who can't sleep because of nightmares of war. And from one distressed army wife, I am informed of economic hardships. "Do you know my husband is paid so little," she writes, "that we qualify for food stamps?" Another woman, a doctor whose children went through Berkeley on ROTC scholarships, confides at the end of her letter, "You see, their father was a marine who was killed in Vietnam."

Even many of the sarcastic but revealing comments from infantrymen contain overtones of suffering. "I hope you sleep well tonight," writes one father. "I too would like to sleep at home with my wife. We have a baby on the way but I am being shipped thousands of miles away."

Finally, there are a number of men who write of the lives they save, those of Serbs and Albanians in the Kosovo conflict.

We are good people living hard lives: this is their theme. "We risk our lives that you can have the academic freedom to attack your military protectors." Resentment of civilians and especially academics "in the ivory tower" is another theme echoed throughout the communications.

To those who have shared a part of their lives with me, I send personal responses geared toward the realities they face. "I am not trying to attack people in the military," I might say, "only the military industrial complex itself and its impact on the university. There are many good people in the military, and you sound like one of them. I am a Quaker myself and against war." Judging by follow-up correspondence, Quakers receive a measure of respect in military circles. "I just wanted to know where you were coming from," commented one writer. "I respect your religious views; recall my original message," said another. Among the most well-meaning responses, I have received invitations from public relations departments and other authorities for tours of West Point, the Air Force Academy in Colorado, and even a submarine voyage.

The most moving telephone call (admittedly, most of these calls were far from moving) came from a gay ex-army captain who had been forced to choose between his career and his lover. Talking to me marked a turning point in his life, he said. He went from despondent to agreeing to check out a career in social work in the course of his call.

The most compelling story came in the form of a confession from a Department of Defense employee, formerly an enlisted man:

> I served in the Army for four years, including the Gulf War. I have been a witness and culprit to the wanton destruction of the environment. The cost of repairs, some of which are irreversible, ranges in the millions of dollars not to mention the intangible consequences such as how the locals tend to view the American military in their village (e.g., Somalia).
>
> Your letter which is being circulated around the DoD along with a copy of the rebuttal of some foolish young officer is being used to further lionize the role of the military in today's global environment and our invaluable service to our nation's mission. I understand that you were not questioning the moral fabric of those who serve. Keep the faith!

Seeking Peace
in the Community

In the first article in this section, Sharon Buttry shows how she sought her way forward moment by moment in a threatening situation. FRIENDS JOURNAL has many such testimonies in its pages—a response to being accosted on a dark street as a woman almost reaches her home, jostling and threatening behavior by a group of young men toward another as he seeks medicine for a suddenly ill child on another dark night. One Friend tells the readers that he learned, with the example of more experienced Friends, to experience calmness in the midst of a peace demonstration that had become too aggressive. All rely on the sense of meeting within themselves and on nonviolent moves that they have learned in workshops, although they may have thought during the workshop that they would probably never need such techniques in their daily experience.

There are many ways to witness to peace. Individuals are led to one that fits their personality and preparation. Alaine Duncan, for example, follows a leading to use skills and contacts that she already knows well to provide a potent service for veterans. Although Alaine disagrees with the war that the soldiers had been fighting, she cherishes the persons and helps them to heal.

Early Friends thought that the "magistrate," as they called men we would today call policemen, should never be directed to move against anyone for religious reasons. They believed that any church and the authority of the government should be completely divorced. They believed the magistrates served in many times and places, however, where there was less clarity about their roles and Friends' right relationships to those roles. Some Friends thought at times that although Friends could not carry arms, the magistrates could. Some Friends thought that the power of armed magistrates should be used to defend settlers and citizens. Others questioned having the magistrates carry arms, and more particularly, being protected by armed men when they themselves would not carry arms. The honesty of magistrates was, also, often questioned. In his article, "Police and Community: Building Peace," Paul Hamell takes up many of the issues we have with policing today. Hamell gives to issues of policing the integrity and seriousness of thought that it deserves. It is an issue to which Friends may find they are increasingly drawn. The idea of community policing has been extended recently from citizen patrols in U.S. villages and cities into ideas of "just policing" internationally, policing that might provide practical steps as alternatives to war.[1] One way to start thinking about "just policing" might be for Friends to study the "International Declaration of Human Rights" and to discuss what they see as its implications for peacemaking.

The next two short selections present current work that Friends have been doing to reconcile their religious belief, as stated in a New York Yearly Meeting minute of 2006, given in the text, with possible actions that Friends might take to witness to their belief that paying for war is against the religious conscience of many Friends. This, too, is an issue on the international level as well as on an individual and national level. And, just as with any of the above approaches to peacemaking, witness begins in spiritual clarity.

A recent peace movement that Friends have joined is Restorative Justice. Bette Rainbow Hoover's essay on "Restorative Practices as Practical Peacemaking" is quite rich in that it combines the ideas of using Restorative Justice in local schools and courts to resolve local problems, and in local ways of bringing diverse citizens together to discuss international tensions. It also points to ways of using Restorative Justice to resolve international conflicts to avert war. To the list of resources Anthony Manousos provides us, I would add Gerald W. Schlabach's book *Just Policing, Not War*.

And finally, in this section, Joe Peacock, in "Scattering Seeds in International Peace Work," gives us a glimpse of his experience as one of many Friends who leave their homes and families to carry out Friends' work and witness for peace around the globe. FOR (Fellowship of Reconciliation) and IFOR (International Fellowship of Reconciliation) both involve many Friends. Many Friends also participate in such groups as CPT (Christian Peacemakers Teams) and PBI (Peace Brigades Inter-

---

[1] Gerald W. Schlabach, ed. *Just Policing, Not War: An Alternative Response to World Violence* (2007).

---

national), both of which serve worldwide. Then there are the Friends' groups, such as AFSC (American Friends Service Committee), which has a presence in many countries, and FPT (Friends Peace Teams), which have been serving actively in volatile or post war areas. FPT includes AGLI (African Great Lakes Initiative), II (the Indonesian Initiative), and the PLA (Peacebuilding en las Americas). FPT facilitators use AVP workshops extensively, training local people to carry on the workshops themselves. They also have been developing by study and by trial and error ways of working with the trauma that follows natural disasters and wars. In AGLI, such programs have been called HROC (Healing and Reconciling Our Communities). Most of these groups have very little overhead; all have volunteers. These volunteers rely on clearness committees to make certain that the work continues to be spiritually grounded and reasonably focused.

S.H.

January 2005

A Response to a Mugging

by Sharon A. Buttry

The morning was Friday, hot and muggy; the month July. I was in the parking lot of Friendship House, a community action organization that I direct, in an inner city neighborhood of Detroit, Michigan. The double side doors of my Ford Universal van were open and I was inside cleaning up, in anticipation of guests who were to arrive for a tour of Hamtramck, a neighborhood in Detroit, later in the day. I turned around to see a man, about 30 years old, with a gun. He pointed the gun at my stomach and demanded all my money. It was one of those moments when a million things go through your mind. I have always prayed that if I were ever faced with a violent situation, I would be able to respond in a way that is consistent with my conviction for nonviolent action.

I was frightened but sensed a calm in my spirit that was, I believe, God's gift to me at that moment. I quickly assessed the situation. The man smelled of alcohol but he was not agitated or overly aggressive. I guessed that he did not want to attract attention from the other people driving through the parking lot. I clearly remembered a piece of non-violence training: If you can engage your enemy in a common task, the distraction may lead to a humane interaction. It was as if a voice inside me was giving me wisdom for the moment.

So, I said: "You know, I only have $1 in my purse; but here, let's look through my purse together."

The man climbed into the van with me and laid his gun down on the seat. He undid one zipper, I undid another; we searched until we found the bill I knew was in my purse. He sat down on the floor of the van with his legs dangled out on the pavement. He started to cry.

"Is this your first time?" I asked. He nodded his head "yes." I thought, is he putting on an act? I tested my theory.

"Look," I said, "I am a minister; I work here at Friendship House. We are here to help. Why are you crying?"

He cried harder and told me how he had really messed this up and what a mess his life was. His mom had died four months earlier and his world had fallen apart. He lost his job, was terribly depressed, and had come to this, attempting a robbery. He had an 11-year-old daughter and was ashamed of how he was unable to care for her in his state of grief and depression. We talked for 40 minutes.

I kept handing him tissues and he got all his grief out. He hadn't talked to anyone about his feelings, not even his father, from whom he had stolen the gun.

I asked him if his mother was a praying woman. "Yes," he said, and I suggested we pray together about getting his life together. He closed his eyes, but I didn't. We had a prayer.

Afterwards we made a plan. I promised that I would not call the police as long as he did two things: return the gun to his father and tell him what happened today; and come back to meet with me about finding a job, without being under the influence of alcohol.

We agreed and I started to relax. He was quiet for a minute then panicked. "You are going to call the police when I leave, aren't you?"

"George, I am not. You have a daughter and you can't take care of her from jail. You are just going to have to trust me."

We talked some more and he asked me if I could forgive him. I assured him I could. We exchanged names and phone numbers and agreed to meet on Monday. He got up to leave, got halfway across the parking lot, then turned around and came back. "Are you sure you forgive me?" he asked again. "Yes, with God's help, I forgive you." "You know what I really need?" he asked. "What do you really need?" (I thought he was going to ask me for a cigarette!)

"I need a hug." So I gave him a hug and, reassured, he walked away. He called me later that day to thank me again, for forgiving him!

We met the next week, and about six weeks later we were able to find George a job. He reported to me that he went home and talked to his dad that Friday. Togeter, with George's sister, they talked and grieved together, something they had not been able to do when his mom had died. George was amazed at the healing he felt in his family relationships. We worked together to get his dad into the food bank program operated by Friendship House, something he qualfied for as a senior with low income. George spent some time volunteering at the food bank and hanging out with the men there who offer the love and friendship of God as part of their volunteer work. One of them even took George out to lunch a couple of times.

George has had several jobs since then; but whenever he comes to pick up food for his dad, he always gives me a hug. It was the mugging that turned into a hugging.

November 2008

Courageously Faithful: Bringing Peace to War

by Alaine D. Duncan

I am a Quaker
I am a Taoist, Buddhist, Christian Quaker.
I am an acupuncturist
A trauma therapist
A peace activist
A healer.

Early every Wednesday morning, I sit in gathered silence in the belly of Walter Reed Army Medical Center. I sit with a group of acupuncturists and body-workers. Our Restore and Renew Wellness Clinic will treat around 70 nurses and doctors, social workers and chaplains, administrators and orderlies, physical therapists and food service workers—civilians and soldiers. We bring peace to the very tangible experience of war that soldiers bring home with them and give unknowingly and unbidden to their caregivers.

And on every Thursday morning, I travel to the Veterans Administration Hospital—to their War-Related Illness and Injury Study Center, where I serve as an acupuncturist, using needles as an instrument of peace for veterans of war.

Each day and in every treatment I call on Abba—Father God for his bedrock of protection, safety, and forgiveness. I call on Amma—Mother God for her peace in the quiet, dark places, for her mysterious gift of healing, for her unboundaried presence. I feel their presence fill the room—and it carries my words, my hands, my needles.

Together Abba-Amma, Mother-Father God, welcomes home warriors, forgives them the sins of war, and heals wounds in the bodies and souls of soldiers, of soldiers and their nurses, soldiers and their lovers, soldiers and their children, soldiers and their chaplains.

How did this work come to be the pivot around which my mind and heart revolve? What have I learned that is worthy to share in the context of Faithful Courage?

In the fall of 2004 I "happened" to hear Kevin and Joyce Lucey interviewed on the radio. Their son, Lance Corporal Jeffrey Lucey, had come home from Iraq in 2003. Unable to cope with what he had seen, and what he had been asked to do, he committed suicide. His dad is a social worker, his mom a nurse. He couldn't have asked for more active, involved, or loving parents.

My first thought: acupuncture could have made a difference for this young man, and for his family—what a shame the Veterans Administration wasn't set up to offer it to him. I was filled with a feeling, a knowing, that it didn't have to be this way for Jeff or for his family. I lost that thought in the day-to-day of life until, three months later, I again "happened" to hear the Luceys interviewed.

This time I woke up—I said to myself, "I am the director of a complementary healing center; I am in a position to bring together a group of healers who can make a difference for soldiers, their families, and their caregivers." It was a leading, and it picked me up.

We birthed our nonprofit affiliate, Crossings HealingWorks, with a mission to "bring ancient healing traditions that restore and renew the body, mind, and spirit of people touched by trauma—creating peace for one family, one community, one world—one person at a time."

Did it take courage? Yes—I hid my three-pointed hat, took the bumper stickers off my car, and went undercover with my teeth chattering the first few times I walked through the gates of Walter Reed. What if I was found out? Would they cast me out? Ridicule me? Court-martial me? Worse yet—Google me?

Did it take faithfulness? Yes—this is something I have learned about leadings. They carry us past, over, and through our fear. It was no longer an option for me to not engage in a deeply personal way with people wounded by war. My leading to do this work helped me transcend the "us and them" dichotomy that exists not only between Quakers and the military—but between those of us who are "outside the gates" with those of us who live and work "inside the gates."

This is a different kind of peace work. I never thought I was doing enough for peace because I wasn't doing big things—like organizing massive demonstrations. Now I have discovered that the small act of placing a small needle in the small ear of an Army medic at Walter Reed is absolutely and unequivocally peace work. I have discovered that not only is it okay to work for peace within my domain—it is my calling to work for peace within my domain and not someone else's domain. I have found what I call my divine enough. Between God and me, it's enough; I am enough. I have found my divine enough.

I have immersed myself in the study of trauma. I have learned something of how it impacts our body/mind/spirit—and how we heal from the disorganization it creates. My goals?

• To keep these folks out of the criminal justice system—an important task, since we know that unresolved trauma is a principal cause of violent, impulsive acts. Traumatic reenactment is one way our unconscious minds attempt to complete and bring closure to life-threatening experiences.

• To keep these folks in healthy relationships with their children—an important task, since we know that the children of parents who are so traumatically frozen that they can't gaze lovingly into their infants' eyes have higher rates of drug abuse and suicide than those whose parents made a visual and tactile connection with them as infants. This is how the dynamics of trauma get passed on in families.

• To help these folks make thoughtful, flexible, creative contributions in our political discourse—decisions that are not straight-jacketed and molded by fear sold cheap by our political leaders.

I've learned a few things, and have lots more to learn.

I've learned that the impact of war is not limited to the persons who served, their time of service, or the geographic borders of their service. Their caregivers, their families, their communities—our whole nation is impacted by soldiers coming home and bringing the trauma of war home with them. Trauma is a vibrational illness, and it is catching—like the flu. I have also been heard to say that recovery from trauma is equally catching—it spreads like honey on warm toast.

In the face of trauma, our neurological systems go on high alert. We flee, fight, or freeze. The response we make is highly variable and dependent on how our Creator wired our unique neurological systems. Some of us are made to fight—we are she-bears, we charge when attacked, and others are made to flee—we are white-tailed deer, we run and get out of the way. Still others become immobilized and freeze—we are opossums. It is not better to be a she-bear, a white-tailed deer, or an opossum—we all are part of creation, and we are wired to survive.

The most primitive parts of our brains govern our survival responses; it is not under our conscious control. Our response has nothing to do with our valor, honor, dignity, compassion, or our value as a human being. Our cognitive minds play no role in these decisions; they are not engaged, nor are they useful to our survival when we are facing danger.

We cannot will our fight/flight/freeze response away, we cannot educate it away, we cannot pretend it doesn't exist and be in meaningful dialogue about violence or passivity in our families and communities, about war and peace at home or abroad. We wouldn't really want to lose our fight response, anyway—it is what allows a 110-pound woman to lift an automobile off her child.

When I think about the query, "Do my actions serve to take away the root cause of war?" I think about this primitive survival response. How do my actions help to bring some measure of freedom to this primitive instinct? I say: unwinding, transforming, releasing stuck trauma responses in the body/mind/spirit of individuals who have experienced war is fundamental to finding peace in our families, communities, and world.

A story: "Joe" is a nuclear, biological, and chemical warfare specialist. He was fresh home from Iraq. He had migraine headaches and ruptured discs in his neck from carrying armor. He described his sleep by saying, "I flip-flop like a fish on a pier." He admitted to using alcohol to excess in order to sleep and to medicate his nightmares.

He knew that as a Christian his task was to love others, and he named his job as a soldier to be a necessary evil—he used his forefinger and thumb to demonstrate picking off people behind furniture in my treatment room. He appeared dissociated and disconnected—frozen—as he described this.

His primary complaint was having lost 70 percent of his vision in his left eye due to a retinal bleed. He was also concerned that his memory was not what he knew it to be.

Difficulty sleeping is very common for trauma survivors, as are nightmares. The stress chemicals that help us to be alert to danger get frozen and stuck on high alert and don't turn off easily. Protective at one time in our past, they now get in the way of sleep and healing. Helping to thaw that freeze and find internal peace and quiet is part of trauma recovery.

Symptoms in the head and neck are also very common in trauma. We use our sense organs to orient to trauma, and that orienting response leaves us hyper-vigilant. It is common for people to grind their teeth, have neck pain or restricted range of motion in their necks, ringing in their ears, or eye symptoms after trauma.

These are some of my notes:

"I'm like a turtle—slow, still, quiet." (*Where do you feel that?*)
"In my chest."
"When I'm not a turtle—I'm a dragon—fire, fighting, hot." (*Touch into the edge of that.*)
"Also in my chest."
(He discharges with some light trembling and shaking in the liver and gallbladder meridians in his legs.)
"When I make contact with my spiritual self I feel expanded in my chest and more like a man. My legs are lighter and my shoulders are relaxed."
"I'd like to poke a needle in my eye to let the blood out." (*See yourself doing that.*)
"I'm a beekeeper—calm, resistant to stinging." (*Feel that feeling.*)
"I feel so different in my psyche since coming home. I'm trying to come back. People have me in a groove and I'm different. Some parts of me I like and some I don't. I don't feel at home. I'm trying to come home."
"My skin feels like dragon skin—it's hot and tight." (*Feel that.*)
"I'm going to turn it over to God." (*Feel that; take your time.*)
"My skin feels new, it's cool and green and full of life." (*Feel that.*)
"There's a bubble in my belly—it wants to rise, I feel like laughing and smiling. It's all so ridiculous. I want to send this feeling to my wife." (*Feel that.*)

This is over the course of four sessions. I used acupuncture points primarily on his liver and gallbladder pathways—meridians that run from the eye, across the head in multiple bands, down the neck, and on down to the foot along the outside of our bodies, and then up the inside of the leg and to the chest. They help us with our vision—both our eyes and our mind's eye; with our ability to see a new future. They help our emotions move smoothly, past life's obstacles that might otherwise leave us frustrated and angry. They help soothe and settle stuck fight responses. Some of the points I used had names like Loathsome Jaws, Wilderness Mound, Sun and Moon, Suspended Regulator, Bright and Clear, Chapter Gate, Rooted Spirit, Flowing Valley, and Gate of Hope.

His last session—his eye had recovered, his memory was better, he was sleeping, and he felt more relaxed overall.

He had interviewed for a position with the Strategic War Command: cloth napkins, crystal glassware, and a six-figure salary. He was bubbling over, talking fast. I asked him to slow down and check in with his body. How did he feel when he was there?

"Numb in my head, pain in my belly" (he points to his liver) "and I want to get drunk." (*Feel that.*)
"Those people are crazy." (*Feel that.*)
"It's not for me—I don't belong there." (*Feel that.*)
"I feel a lump in my throat." (*Feel that.*)
He begins to tear up. He wants to cry and scream. I encourage him to see himself screaming as loud as he needs to and crying as much as he needs to—silently.
He's a pretty stoic guy.
He says "Profanity" and holds his head in his hands and weeps.
He says "Violence" and holds his head in his hands and weeps.
He says "Rage" and holds his head in his hands and weeps.
He says "Killing" and holds his head in his hands and weeps.
He says "Grief" and holds his head in his hands and weeps.
He says "Loss" and holds his head in his hands and weeps.
We sit quietly for a time.
He speaks of his fear of meeting others' expectations, of the rejection:
"Who will I be to the world of violence if I am not violent?"
"When I am here, I am more powerful than all the world's armies."
"I feel hope for the first time in a long time."
"I am a simple man who no one can see."

He left the army. He left a $400,000 retirement package and the possibility of a very cushy job at the Pentagon. He went home to the Midwest to be a spiritual leader for his four children. He went to tend his bees and go back to his civilian job.

He told me he was going to write to the Dalai Lama to ask him how to heal his karma. I don't know if he ever did—I think he healed his karma on that day.

He sent me this poem a couple of weeks later:

The Simple Man

I am a simple man.
No one can see me.
Sometimes a few see me. I was born green.
When I am hidden, is when I am most visible.

I am more powerful than all the world's armies.
I can kill you but I choose not to.
My body strikes like the leopard, or my mind.
Hands you a blossoming flower.
Go slowly. Your time for peace is near.
I am a simple man.
I will stop the tears and bring a joyful silence.

Friends, this is peace work. This is the grittiest, grimiest, dirtiest, and most meaningful peace work I have ever done—in the shattered hearts and minds of the veterans of war.

The ancient Chinese said that life happens in a dynamic tension between opposites. Let's look at "courageously faithful."

Courage. Do you hear the Latin root for heart, cour, in courage? Courage belongs to the heart. The heart belongs to the fire element—fire is summer, passion, expansion, connection, fullness, love. Fire is yang.

Faithful. Faithfulness belongs to the water element, to the kidney, to the winter, to the questions, "Do I have enough crop stored away? How long will the cold last? Will I survive?" Water is cold, contemplative, quiet, interior, wise. Water is yin.

Fire without water to temper it burns wildly—like the wildfires we have witnessed out West. Water without fire to warm it is inert, frozen. Neither lives without the other.

Courage cannot live separately from faithfulness any more than the front of your hand can exist without the back of your hand. All courage without faithfulness is a bull in a china shop on a manic episode; all faithfulness without courage is an icicle in a very cold, dark cave.

Life happens in dynamic tension between water and fire, yin and yang, between courage and faithfulness, war and peace—two poles, one life force.

There is a structure in our aorta called the respiratory sinus node. The Chinese called it by its acupuncture point name: Within the Breast. It governs the electrical current that brings coherence and relationship between our breath and heartbeat. It is profoundly impacted by overwhelming life events. Those of you who have experienced automobile accidents, falls, or other jangling events may remember your heart racing or your breath becoming quite shallow. This is part of a whole-body response that allows you to survive what your body perceived to be life-threatening.

When we find our way to safety—in our bodies, not in our intellects—there is greater congruence between our heartbeat and our breath—and there is greater congruence between our heartbeat, our breath, and the generation of alpha waves in our brains. Alpha waves are highly correlated with states of compassion, empathy, creativity, and serenity.

The Chinese use the same character for heart and mind. They know that when we are troubled in our hearts, we are also troubled in our minds—and that peacefulness in our hearts brings peacefulness in our minds.

When I have a greater sense of internal coherence, when I am embodied, present, feeling safe—when my heart is beating peacefully in the kingdom of my body—my brain generates alpha waves, and—this is important, so listen closely: My heart entrains your brain's creation of alpha waves—if we are touching or in close proximity. My peaceful heart entrains your brain to create electrical currents that are highly correlated with states of compassion, empathy, creativity, and serenity.

Our Restore and Renew Wellness Clinic at Walter Reed has treated over 1,100 members of their staff—that is, 15 percent of their 7,000 members. More than 300 have come five times or more. Each one goes back to work with a more peaceful heart, a quieter mind, a more coherent energy system. Each one goes back to work as an alpha wave machine—carrying vibrations of compassion, empathy, creativity, and serenity to their patients and their patients' moms, dads, lovers, and children.

Friends—this is peace work.

Being fully present with each other, in embodied states of love and compassion, affects our biology and our energy field. It creates more order, more flexibility, more balance in the electrical currents that guide our nervous system and all the nervous systems we touch. Trauma resolution spreads like honey on warm toast.

Small things done in big ways. A smile. A hug. Care-filled and thoughtful listening. Being embodied, present, living from our experience of safety rather than our fear helps to create more peaceful, creative, compassionate vibrations in the minds of the people close to us.

Who do you think of as other—and can you find your way to being embodied, present, engaged when you are with them?

Who do you think of as other—and can you find a way to be in your embodied experience of safety when you are with them?

Who do you think of as other—and can you meet them outside of judging their trauma response as inferior or superior to yours?

Who can you find to create a peace-filled vibration with that can quite literally change the world?

What is your domain?

What is a small thing you can do in a big way for peace within your domain?

What is your divine enough?

January 2005

Police and Community: Building Peace

by Paul Hamell

L ate one night in March 2001, in Hackensack, New Jersey, two young men—reputed gangsters and lifelong buddies—got into an argument. One shot the other dead.

The next night, at about the same time, the survivor stood in the street in front of the house where the murder had occurred and began firing an assault rifle into the house. Officers of the Hackensack and Bergen County police departments quickly arrived and, keeping their distance, surrounded the shooter, using what cover and concealment they could find. They repeatedly ordered and begged the shooter to drop his weapon, without returning his ongoing fire.

The shooter retreated up the block, still firing at officers. As he neared the end of the block and the perimeter that was to contain him, he passed within a few yards of two county officers who were concealed in shadows with very little cover. Recognizing their peril, the two officers returned fire, initiating a barrage from all around. The young man went down.

One of the nearby officers walked quietly forward and, as he reached for the fallen man's rifle to remove it, the wounded man lifted the weapon and fired one shot, point-blank, at the officer's head. It narrowly missed. The return barrage that followed ended the gunman's resistance and life.

The two county officers who were at the center of the violence never returned to duty—both retired on psychological disabilities. A third county officer retired on psychological disability some time later, citing this incident as a large part of the stress that was preventing him from continuing as a police officer. Two of the city officers who participated also applied for disability retirement, although I never heard the outcomes of their cases. So let's take the ended careers, disrupted lives, and ongoing anguish of these police officers and their families, and add it to the two dead young men (for the original murder is certainly part of this story) and the suffering of their families and the community that witnessed this violence. What can we make of this?

The sad truth is that within the paradigm our society currently uses in thinking about policing itself, this is a feel-good story. The police demonstrated a gentleness and restraint that is heroic, then demonstrated their goodness again through their suffering. Only the criminal was directly harmed by police use of force, and, after the precipitating murder, no innocents were physically harmed.

The further sad truth is that, in many ways, this story is an aberration. The officers' hesitancy to use force when confronted with a heavily armed assailant who was firing wildly was contrary to their training, and it endangered bystanders who might have been hit by rifle fire penetrating the walls of their homes.

To further complicate this story, on reflection, it seems clear that this was a case of what is sometimes called "suicide by cop." The only explanation I have been able to conceive for the actions of the young man with the rifle is that he had decided to die. Most likely, he understood that the only options left to him were to spend the next 20 years or more in prison or to die. Apparently, he decided to go out in what he regarded as a blaze of glory, and maybe take a cop or two with him to boot.

William L. Hanson, in "Police Power for Peace" (FRIENDS JOURNAL Aug. 2004), wrote about the ambivalence Friends feel toward the police, recognizing the need and obligation for society to exercise control over those of its members who are unable or unwilling to refrain from hurtful actions, while reluctant to endorse the frequent use of force and periodic violence this requires. This story I have told seems to highlight the important areas of concern: the tendency of violence to escalate; the harm to vanquished, victor, and community; and the ultimate necessity of deadly force in the name of society. What makes this story particularly meaningful is the uncommon aversion to the use of deadly force that this particular group of police officers demonstrated. They took extraordinary risks with the safety of themselves and others to avoid killing; but, in the end, they had to kill. One can readily conclude that there is an irreducible need for the use of deadly force in the defense of society; this is as good as it can be.

Friends may find this difficult to accept. I don't think they have to; this apparent need can, at the very least, be reduced substantially.

In his essay, William Hanson expressed a concern about the violence that society uses to protect us and suggested that the solution may lie in developing low-force weapons and tactics for the police, and in further applying the principles of community policing. I share his concern. While I think he is looking in the right direction for tactical solutions, my 27 years as a police officer tell me that the problem is bigger than he indicated and the obstacles to solutions more daunting.

The essence of the problem is that force, either employed or explicitly or implicitly threatened, is the foundation of law enforcement. Citizens must and will comply, regardless. Furthermore, U.S. culture values forcefulness and the decisive use of power; this is reflected in our political rhetoric and the official policies it generates. These values are even more important in the unique subculture of police. As a police officer and manager, I have been explicitly trained to believe that, in a crisis, any decision—even a wrong decision—is better than no decision at all, and to believe its corollary: that any action—even the wrong action—is better than inaction. Waiting and talking are viewed as inaction.

Police are trained and retrained frequently in laws governing the use of force. This is obviously a good thing, but it means that (for instance) in New Jersey every officer will be told twice a year, "There is no duty to retreat for law enforcement officers. You may press forward, overcoming force with force to attain a lawful objective. . . . The force you see coming at you is the force you can use; if you see deadly force coming at you, you may use deadly force."

The police are also extensively trained and retrained in using deadly force; they spend a lot of time on the shooting range. For very good reasons, they are taught always to think about potential dangers, to regard anyone they don't know well as a potential assailant, to position themselves defensively, and to have a plan. In other words, a police officer's mental world is full of danger and violence.

The bottom line is that our police live in a world where decisive action and force are normal ways to get things done, and where violence is to be expected. Not only is this acceptable to society, it is entirely logical. I can't argue with the logic.

Yet, many Quakers regard this as wrong; they know it experimentally, as well as from Scripture.

It's not society's logic that is to be questioned; it's the assumptions. If one embraces the assumption explicit in our laws that force, and even deadly violence, are acceptable when employed against equivalent un-lawful force, then current practice makes sense. If one begins with other assumptions, different outcomes will follow.

If we assume that violence is never acceptable—not even in defense of an individual or society—then any violent act becomes intolerable. Not that we should send people to prison for acting in self-defense or defense of others; rather, we should change the way we think about this.

If forcibly restraining someone from harming another or oneself is an act of love, then not to act protectively is a failure to show love.

If I choose nonresistance for myself and accept whatever dangers that might imply for me, I may be acting out of love. But if I ask another to protect me, but not to defend him- or herself, I am being selfish.

If we accept that it is wholly unfair for society to ask a few of its members to be responsible for the safety of all and to place themselves in dangerous situations where they may have to use violent means or die, we must do all we can to reduce these risks, or we are not acting in love.

So, our best beginning would be to find a way to reduce the amount and intensity of violence directed against the police. Fortunately, the leading cause of violence in the United States is widely agreed on and unlikely to generate partisan debates about economic justice—it is drugs. Alcohol, crack, PCP, and the like make people violent and irrational. Alcohol alone is a leading cause of violence. Illegal drug trade also possesses a special power for generating violence; this was true of alcohol prohibition, and it is true of other prohibited drugs.

Our streets seem unsafe and our prisons are full because our response to the challenge of drugs has been misdirected. We have been engaged in a "war" on illegal drugs for decades now, and the problem has only continued to grow. After decades of energetic enforcement, anyone who wants drugs can still get them without much difficulty. It should be clear by now that, to borrow a phrase, "War is not the answer." Prohibition has failed us for the second time in a century, and it is time to look for a response to drugs that will work.

Taking the drug trade out of the hands of criminals should immediately reduce the level of violence. It would also free up enormous resources now dedicated to the bloated criminal justice system—resources that would then be available for other responses to drugs and violence that might be more effective. They could hardly be less effective.

If police were not tasked with forcefully eradicating drug use from a society that insists on using drugs, police could again be seen (and see themselves) as part of that society, rather than as an overstretched occupying army. The aggressive policing that results from the assignment to fight a losing war exacerbates racial profiling, and it leads to other police practices seen as harassment by the community, including excessive force and mistakes that the police make with their guns.

When the police rejoin the community, the community can truly take responsibility for its own safety. This is the essential concept behind community policing, which is the most promising idea in law enforcement. Unfortunately, too many police departments have outwardly embraced the concept, then assigned its implementation to a self-contained community policing bureau, which, without the involvement of the entire department, cannot be more than a public relations office. Some have set up separate community policing units that have been used as aggressive street crime and narcotics suppression teams, rather than partners in peacemaking with the community.

True community policing will mean shared responsibility for keeping the community safe. If our communities accept this responsibility, the first step will be reducing the abuse of intoxicants. Then, with these primary causes of violence being addressed outside of the criminal justice system, communities and police can cooperate in reducing actual violence and other threats to safety and security. The police can again move toward being seen by all communities as friends and protectors.

It should be apparent by this point that developing low-force weapons and tactics is only the simpler part of solving the problem. And here, we do not have to begin from scratch; there are many places to look for ideas that are already working. It is incongruous that a mentally ill person who becomes violent in a hospital will be restrained by staff members equipped with mattresses and heavy blankets, while a person who becomes violent on the street will be restrained by police officers equipped with aluminum clubs, chemical sprays, and guns. Surely we can apply what we already know.

Another place to look is in other countries with less tolerance of violence. The United Kingdom is one such place; the British are unwilling to accept an armed police force in their midst. Of course, police who protect likely terrorist targets in Britain are armed, and a few patrol cars do have guns locked in safes in the trunk, but, outside of airports and a few parts of London, it is very unusual to see an armed police officer.

One consequence of this is that British police receive far more training in unarmed defense and control techniques than most of their U.S. counterparts do. They are better at avoiding the need for extreme violence.

Another consequence is that only a few highly screened and trained, experienced officers are permitted to deploy firearms, and the conditions for deploying them are more restrictive. In the United States, every police officer knows that the appropriate response to a suspect armed with a knife is the officer's sidearm; in the United Kingdom, the mandated response is a non-lethal Taser.

After almost three decades in policing, I know that neither the U.S. public nor its police are ready to embrace the idea of an unarmed constabulary. However, I have come to believe that this should be our goal. The greatest obstacles to change within the law enforcement community are cultural, and the omnipresence of guns poisons the culture with violence. Guns exist to be used.

The police officers whose moment of horror opened this article are my friends; indeed, after almost 30 years in the business, all police officers are my friends. I have known one of the officers at the center of the story, one who never came back to work, for 25 years. He is a Vietnam War veteran who had gotten over his nightmares of battle many years ago. A few seconds in Hackensack brought it all back to him, and it was a long time before he slept again.

The relationship between domestic peace and international peace that William Hanson wrote of is embodied in my friend. It may be that to bring peace to the world, we have to work outward in widening circles, finding peace for ourselves, then our neighbors and communities, then our country and the world. We will find, as Friends have always known, that there are no discrete issues of social or international policy to wrestle with—everything is interrelated. It all just comes down to making God's love manifest in the world.

Why Pray for Peace and Pay for War?

by Steve Leeds

Friends challenge their governments and take personal risks in the cause of peace. We urge one another to refuse to participate in war as soldiers, or as arms manufacturers. We seek ways to support those who refrain from paying taxes that support war. We work to end violence within our own borders, our homes, our streets, and our communities. We support international order, justice, and understanding.

—*Faith and Practice, Pacific Yearly Meeting, 2001.*

An internal conflict has been seething within me for years. I prayed repeatedly that it would just go away. As a citizen of this country and of the world, I tried to do everything possible to promote peace. I prayed, wrote letters, organized, marched, committed civil disobedience, and more. Every year, as winter turned to spring and April 15 approached, I felt dread grip me. How could I not only pray and work for peace and justice, but also take a public stand and stop paying for war?

These are the painful and complicated dilemmas that challenge Quaker believers in peace and justice who love life and care for our natural world. There are many opportunities for us as well.

I have symbolically refused to pay the federal tax on my phone bill since the 1970s. In the mid 1980s I refused to pay my federal withholding taxes, and then painfully watched as my wages, and those of a few other war tax resisters, were garnished—along with penalties and interest. It felt painful and disempowering.

I crumbled. Social conditioning, fear of the Internal Revenue Service, taboos about challenging the government, concerns about economic security, and the lack of a collective war tax resistance strategy in my community led me back to paying my taxes in the late 1980s. I felt there was no other choice. After all, I could be a peace and justice activist and still pay for war. Keeping under the radar on the tax front and giving back as much as I could to my community (the world) became my mantra.

Fifteen years later, through renewed spiritual commitment and membership in a Friends meeting, I was led to take action with other Quakers on war tax resistance. It began among a few of us, and that's all it takes.

Early in 2006, my meeting began cohosting war tax resistance gatherings with Northern California War Tax Resistance. We urged Friends in our meeting to engage in symbolic war tax resistance—refusing federal phone taxes, paying under protest, withholding symbolic amounts, or living below the tax line—and letting our legislators know about it. We found that a number of households in the meeting partook in some form of war tax resistance, symbolic or otherwise.

The wars in Iraq, Afghanistan, and proxy conflicts elsewhere raged on, funded by my tax dollars, and ever more resources paid for death and destruction while growing needs went unfunded here at home. I felt a heightened sense of urgency to resolve the issues that kept me from being a public war tax resister.

Philosophically, it's a slam dunk. No more war. Not with my dollars.

Logistically, though, it's easy to become fixated on the mechanics and legal aspects of war tax resistance. There's a lot to learn and consider. My journey, through discernment, prayer, and the support of others, led me to focus on complex social and financial issues. Mostly, I have been confronting my fear of the IRS and the insecurity of not knowing where this will lead.

In my formative years I was emphatically taught to vote when of age, pay my taxes, and speak up when I disagreed. These values are inculcated in many of us, in our families, throughout the educational system, and socially and institutionally as we move into adulthood. Paying our taxes is seen as a civic duty. It's also an individual and private process between an individual (or couple) and a large, bureaucratic entity, the Internal Revenue Service. It makes most taxpayers feel quite powerless. For millions of us, handing over our hard-earned dollars for the good and the not-so-good—for needed social programs, the operation of government bureaucracies, and the fueling of the war machine—is simply a fact of life. The phrase Thomas Jefferson coined, "There are two certainties in life, death and taxes," is a stark and true reality.

Fear of losing what financial security I have, worry about how my family and friends will react, and anxiety about what the IRS would do add confusion and doubt. Will I have to reduce my quality of life to be a tax resister? What are my responsibilities as a family wage earner? What will extended family members think? What about my larger community of friends when my resistance becomes public?

I am fortunate in this regard to be single and a renter with some savings and retirement benefits. Still, I have needed to face family and friends—some supportive; some not, some withholding judgment through silence or making jokes. I would like their understanding and support, but I have little control over the reactions of others.

My choice to be a war tax resister means that I will continue to grapple with these issues. There are no easy answers. I often reflect about those living on the streets in the neighborhood of our meetinghouse, in Iraq and Afghanistan, and in so many other places. There is no easy way to do this. But I am glad to grapple with all the turmoil, joy, and self-discovery this decision brings forward.

It is the fear factor that has caused the most difficulty in my decision to be a public war tax resister, and not knowing how the government will respond. If 9/11 has taught me anything about our country, it is how many of us were manipulated by that tragic event into becoming terrified of Islam, of al-Qaida, of Iraqi weapons of mass destruction. Fear is real and it can paralyze and poison. When I sit in silent worship, I am aware of how true this is for me, too. I pray that I can, through action, transform my fear into hope.

In fact, these fears pale when I reflect upon what is being done with my tax dollars, 41 percent of which, according to Friends Committee on National Legislation, go for military preparations and war. My doubts slide away when I think about the effects our government policies have on people here at home and around the globe, about my privilege living as a middle-class U.S. citizen, and about my responsibility as a member of the global family of God's creatures.

For the 2006 tax year I have held back $1,040 from the IRS (symbolic of the IRS 1040 form). Living with multiple feelings—fear, joy, and liberation—makes life whole. My faith as a Quaker, striving to be nonviolent and to oppose all wars, has led me down this path. I am sustained by the knowledge that many Quakers throughout history have resisted paying taxes for war. When I think that we as a faith community need to do more, I know that the we starts with me.

Yes, the IRS will get what I owe in taxes, plus more in penalties and late fees. I can afford it. The privilege I enjoy, compared to over half of the world's population who live in dire want, makes me realize that whatever hardship I face is small in comparison. I can truly say I am overjoyed to not pay for war voluntarily.

When April 15 rolls around this year, I expect my experience will lead me to step up again, not only to pray and work for peace, but also to refuse to pay for war.

I am finding hope, though not always easily, in the process of being a war tax resister—in learning more about myself, my intention, my F/ friends, and my community. This is action that will be consistent with my faith and belief in a just, peaceful, and humane future.

March 2008

Yielding to Our Faith:
A Message from a Harmless Quaker

(Excerpt)

by Nadine Hoover

" . . . New York Yearly Meeting reaffirms our faith today:

> The Living Spirit works in the world to give life, joy, peace and prosperity through love, integrity and compassionate justice among people. We are united in this Power. We acknowledge that paying for war violates our religious conviction. We will seek ways to witness to this religious conviction in each of our communities. —NYYM, Fourth Month 2006

Ways to grow into and rediscover a witness to our religious faith and convictions include:

• Encourage your Friends meeting or church or other faith community to write a statement of conscientious objection to paying for war, and deliver that message to your local communities and representatives.

• Write a statement of religious faith and conscience with the support of your faith community, include it with your tax return, and copy it to your local newspaper(s), Congressional representative, senators, faith community, faith publications, local review (draft) board, secretary of the treasury, taxpayer advocacy service, and/or the National Campaign for a Peace Tax Fund (see <www.peacetaxfund.org>). To the National Campaign, include a list of whom you've sent it to, permission to reprint, and a donation to follow-up in Washington, D.C.

• Redirect your taxes, or any portion (the entirety, the percent of military expenditure, or a token amount) to an escrow account to be held in trust for the U.S. government as an act of nonviolent civil initiative. Those adopting this approach may spend time and energy in responding to the IRS and suffer penalties imposed by the government. It is good to form a clearness and support group for this action.

• Work through the courts to establish in law the rights already guaranteed by the First and Ninth Amendments to the Constitution and by international covenants that provide for freedom of religious expression, but continue to be ignored by our current government. Some individuals and a few groups have petitioned the courts to recognize their rights, and you may be able to as well!

• Live below a taxable level. This is an individual choice to either keep income below a taxable bracket or to give away one's income to reduce one's tax liability. Financial and moral supports of others for this witness often make these choices more possible, especially over the long run.

• Withdraw any investments you may have in corporations that profit from war production and service and place your savings in accounts that will support and encourage your local community and purchase from local producers.

• Pursue local ordinances that deny corporations recognition as persons, granting to them the rights of persons, and that deny recognition of corporate charters as contracts, reestablishing the oversight of government to engage in limited activities to benefit the people (contact POCLAD, P.O. Box 246 South Yarmouth, MA 02664, 508-398-1145; and Community Environmental Legal Defense Fund, P.O. Box 2016 Chambersburg, PA 17201, 717-709-0457) since pursuit of excessive inequality in wealth for the few rather than the benefits of all is the driving force of militarism.

I am deeply indebted and grateful to the Living Spirit that illuminates me every day, and to all the members of New York Yearly Meeting's Committee on Conscientious Objection to Paying for War, who inspire and challenge me and offer companionship on this spiritual journey.

July 2008

Restorative Practices as Practical Peacemaking

by Bette Rainbow Hoover

A restorative and holistic approach to peacemaking is urgently needed in a world where violence is an integral part of the fabric of our global community. The media and our elected leaders fan our fears, and we readily slip into defense mode. We sometimes forget Gandhi's living example of his words, "Be the peace you want to see," and Penn's query on seeing what love can do. How can we make a difference? How do we know when our work for peace is effective?

The emerging social movement for Restorative Justice (RJ) offers timely guidance to restore right relationships and take responsibility for our actions—to each other and to our environment. Based on concepts and practices of Indigenous peoples from around the world, the present movement was resurrected in the 1970s. A Canadian, Albert Eglash, is credited with the term *restorative justice* as a form of addressing restitution in the criminal retributive system. To First Nations Canadians, it was already a universal truth that everyone is accountable to the community and that people need to get along in order to survive. That truth is still relevant and still universal.

Ceremony was important in traditional peacemaking practices. In the Americas, ceremonies included shared meals, fasting, vision quests, and sweat lodges. Closure to an agreement could symbolically include rituals such as smoking a pipe, burying a hatchet, or feasting, as described by Evan Pritchard in *The Way of the Heron* (see <www.algonquinculture.org>). Traditional African societies used many similar practices in their peacemaking. Although the particular ceremonies were unique to the group, the intended outcome was the same (as described by Birgit Brock-Utne in *Indigenous Conflict Resolution in Africa*—see <www.africavenir.com>). Uganda's practice, for example, included having all parties drink a bitter herb from the Oput tree to symbolize the bitterness the disagreement caused the community. With the help of elders, all affected parties were brought together to find a resolution that worked for the whole community.

Modern-day circles, in the manner of traditional practices, bring everyone affected by a conflict together to tell our stories and take responsibility for the effects of our behaviors. In a circle guided by a facilitator, an elder, or other respected peacemaker, the group looks for ways to repair damage, heal wounds, and make things better. Together, the stakeholders find solutions that honor themselves and their communities—locally and globally.

Mennonite author Howard Zehr, author of *The Little Book of Restorative Justice*, whose pioneering work provides an understanding of restorative practices, lays out the essential guidelines:

- Who has been hurt?
- What are their needs?
- Whose obligations are these?
- Who has a stake in this situation?
- What is the appropriate process in which to involve stakeholders in an effort to put things right?

These queries are the basis for reframing issues in a wide range of societal violence—beyond the legal justice system where they were first applied.

Women's Peace Exchange 2007

A group of Quaker, Jewish, and Muslim women gathered in autumn of 2006 and decided to invite Israeli and Palestinian women to join them in a women's peace exchange. Grandmothers from Great Britain, who pioneered a Women to Women for Peace organization at the height of the Cold War, were also invited to join the delegation. Skeptics questioned what good such a gathering could do towards a century-old Middle Eastern conflict. Questions were raised about the ability of a small group of women to raise the necessary funds to accomplish such an ambitious task. Organizers of the Women's Peace Exchange 2007: *Nurturing the Seeds of Peace*, remained steadfast in their belief that bringing people together—to face each other—is possible and can make a difference.

Organizers employed a key RJ principle that states: *"Show equal concern and commitment to victims and offenders, involving both in the process of justice."* In the group's initial circle, a safe space was created so stories could be told and healing could begin. Slowly at first, as trust was being built, the truth began to emerge and then erupted. Our Israeli and Palestinian guests, who lived mere miles from each other, discovered their realities were worlds apart. U.S. and British women moved between detachment and guilt for the policies of their countries in the conflict—both historical and present-day. None of us could escape the reality that all of us were affected by this struggle.

How does this affect you? Once the space for dialogue is established and the intention for making things better is agreed upon, participants are ready to ask the hard questions and do some intense self-examination and listening. The participants are invited to begin with the center of their own universe—themselves. As people share their stories and explore their feelings and desires, they discover their common humanity. Through this simple yet profound process, hearts open and bridge-building can begin.

In our initial circle, a Palestinian and a Jewish Israeli woman discovered a similar value: they worried about the safety of their children and wanted the best for them. One had given up a satisfying job in order to be available to her son who had to navigate many Israeli checkpoints each day to and from school. The other agonized over her grandchildren being turned into soldiers and taking part in the occupation. They looked in each other's eyes as they spoke their truths and were each as surprised as the other with what they heard. One chose to teach her children nonviolence in the way of Jesus and Gandhi and the other encouraged her children to leave the country—to save their souls and their lives. Tears and hugs ensued.

Who else is affected and how? Moving from me to thee, restorative practices direct participants to look outside themselves and see who else is hurting and affected by a given situation. As we identify the stakeholders and the needs of the greater community, accountability and responsibility are shared in a wider context.

As our small group of women explored this question regarding life in Israel and the occupied territories, we discovered the myriad of ways we are all affected by the situation. Our families and friends, our faith communities, and our countries were all connected like a giant web. Emotions run raw on this subject and we didn't pretend to have solutions to the problem. All we had was a process and our willingness to take a risk and speak out truth.

What are the unintended consequences of actions and programs? In the process of making peace, we were becoming more aware of our real power and our voices became stronger. We grew into our roles as citizen diplomats. The delegation participated in a panel discussion at a conference called "The Effects of War on Women and the Environment in Israel/Palestine" in Washington, D.C. We ate together, gave each other backrubs, and took walks in the woods. Sometimes we couldn't talk with each other because of perceived differences that in the moment seemed insurmountable. And sometimes we had trouble finding the strength to meet with yet another group of strangers. At these times, we circled up and reminded ourselves of our love for each other and our mutual desire for justice and peace.

Near the end of our time together, we again asked the question of who has been affected. This time the intention of the question was to name all those whom we had touched with our message. The list was robust and seemed endless. We looked at each other in astonishment, knowing that something bigger than us had happened—something that touched each of us profoundly and that *did* make a difference. We knew that many had been moved by our powerful circle of ordinary women.

What can I/we do to make things better? An agreement that emerges from restorative dialogue circle needs to include apologies and acknowledgements of accountability as well as a concrete plan that can be implemented. Since we were all on the same side of the problem by the second week, this question evoked amazing responses that were incorporated in a visionary and yet practical agreement. Our working plan included specific follow-up commitments as well as support for the United Nations Security Council Resolution 1325 for Women, Peace, and Security (see <www.peacewoman.org>). We came to the circle as individuals with our own views of reality and parted as sisters with deeper commitments to justice and peace.

Evaluation and next steps: A careful review of the process is important to learn how to do it better the next time. A focus on what works (rather than what doesn't work) provides an opportunity to create a base on which to build future collaborative work. We all had learned a lot from the experience. Although some things we would do differently the next time, those involved in Women's Peace Exchange 2007, overwhelmingly, responded with something akin to "You bet we'd do it again."

Other Ways Restorative Principles and Practices are Used

Juvenile services in approximately 28 states refer young people for restorative dialogue in lieu of the traditional retributive path. Seen as a type of mediation, the circle expands to include the support system of each youth. Parents and friends, aunts, uncles, or teachers are a part of a process that comes to an agreement deemed as fair and reasonable by everyone involved.

Community conferencing, in the tradition of the Maori peoples of New Zealand, has been practiced in Baltimore, Md., since 1995. The program brings everyone affected by conflict together in a circle to talk with each other and come to resolution. The Center's services are available to a variety of sectors including neighborhoods, criminal justice, law enforcement, schools, and human services. The program is promoted by the campaign for a Department of Peace as a best practice to be replicated. (More information may be found at <www.communityconferencing.org>.)

School systems begin to follow the example of Canada, New Zealand, and Great Britain in using the restorative model instead of expulsion for early offenders. Circle Talk, Rap Circles, and Restorative Dialogue Circles are among the names of the process used for prevention. The facilitated group encourages community building and accountability for behavior among those who participate.

Sulha is the Middle Eastern process of peacemaking that has been revived by a dynamic and diverse group including Israeli Jews, Arabs, and Palestinians. The annual gatherings in Israel bring people of differing views, cultures, and experiences together over several days to share meals, music, and interfaith ritual. Listening circles offer opportunities to understand others and seek solutions. Co-founder Gabriel Meyer says, "We're going to surprise reality until it changes." (For more information, see <www.sulha.com>.)

The Alternatives to Violence Project (AVP) is well-known in Quaker communities as a model birthed in the 1970s for teaching conflict resolution and violence prevention in the prison system. Seated in a circle, participants face each other and engage in dialogue that incorporates some restorative practices—and is often life-changing. Transforming power as a key element in the program offers possibilities for personal change. Practitioners of both AVP and RJ are seeking ways to incorporate core restorative principles in the well-respected model that could bring much needed change to the prison system. (For more information, see Michael Bischoff's article, "How Restorative is AVP? Evaluating the Alternatives to Violence Project according to a Restorative Justice Yardstick," at <www.clarityfacilitation.com>.)

The Native American blessing "All my relations" speaks to the connectedness of all life. Who will speak for the voiceless and the children and the women, the water and the environment? No longer can any of us opt out of our part of a problem—and our responsibility for seeking solutions. Our global village urgently needs us to circle up, heal our hurts, and work together to make things better.

Friends and the Interfaith Peace Movement

by Anthony Manousos

Our country and the world were shaken to the core by the events of September 11, 2001. In response, we were given a moral as well as political choice: to retaliate and seek revenge, or to seek to understand the root causes of violence and find ways to bring about a more peaceful and just world. Sadly, the U.S. government chose the former course. As a result, the world has seen an unrelenting cycle of violence, deception, and mistrust.

But many here in the United States and abroad, seeking a better way, have created an interfaith movement with the potential for reducing, and ultimately ending, the violence attributed to religion. I believe that we as the Religious Society of Friends are called to play an active role in this vital movement. We are a small group, but we have a long tradition of compassionate listening and willingness to speak truth to power. As British Friend Marigold Bentley of Quaker Peace and Social Witness writes:

> The lack of dogma in our own faith enables us to open up to those who, for many, have unacceptable beliefs. Quakers have careful processes to enable delicate spiritual discussions. Quakers also have the gift of meeting-houses across the country that are ideally suited to interfaith encounters as they are unencumbered with religious artifacts. This is used to great effect by many Friends.

This is true in the United States as well as in the United Kingdom. Since 9/11/01, Friends have been eager to become involved in interfaith conversations. When I gave a workshop called "Islam from a Quaker Perspective" at Friends General Conference's Gathering in Amherst, Massachusetts, Friends responded enthusiastically and we were warmly welcomed into the local mosque. At the FGC Gathering in Tacoma, Washington last summer, the Quaker Universalist Fellowship focused on the Interfaith Movement and invited Muslim, Christian, and Jewish speakers to participate.

Friends have also taken part in the interfaith movement at the local level. For many years, interfaith work was primarily carried on by religious leaders and academics. But since 9/11/01, many people now see interfaith work as a matter of urgency for everyone. As British Friend Sylvia Stagg has pointed out, "When I joined the Quaker Committee on Christian and Interfaith Relations (QCCIR), interfaith work was of general interest. Now in 2005 . . . interfaith relations have become an overriding necessity in all our community relations. They are no longer a choice but an absolute necessity."

Most ecumenical organizations, which were mainly founded in the 1950s and 1960s, have changed with the times and became interfaith, enabling Christians, Jews, Muslims, and other religious practitioners to work together as equals in local communities.

Although we, as individuals and as meetings, have reached out warmly and spontaneously to Muslims, Friends are not as involved as we should be in these newly transformed interfaith organizations. Because Friends don't have professional clergy, we have tended to shy away from "organized religion." We have also been excluded from full participation in many ecumenical organizations because we were not considered to be Christian. But times have changed. Today our Quaker voices need to be heard, and we need to listen at these newly emergent interfaith gatherings. Those who feel led to do interfaith work need the support and encouragement of our meetings.

Interfaith work is not without challenges. When we reach out to those who are different, there are apt to be cultural misunderstandings. We need to be tolerant and patient, especially when dealing with Muslims and Jews, who have experienced discrimination and have felt under attack over the centuries. There are many hot-button issues that need to be handled with great care and sensitivity, and we need to do our homework in order to be effective.

The Healing and the Prophetic

Some interfaith groups focus primarily on healing divisions and building understanding. Others advocate for peace and justice. The work that I do for the South Coast Interfaith Council in the Long Beach area is primarily about the former. The mediation skills that I have learned as a Quaker over the past 20 years have proven extremely useful. One of the high points of this past year's program was helping to organize an "interfaith icebreaker" for around 60 teenagers of various faith traditions—no easy task, but deeply rewarding. This summer I am facilitating "interfaith cafes," utilizing the Sacred Listening techniques developed by Kay Lindahl, a local interfaith advocate. Her approach is similar to what we do when we get together as Quakers and have worship sharing. We even use queries to stimulate in-depth conversation in small groups.

The work that I do for Interfaith Communities United for Justice and Peace (ICUJP) often involves "speaking truth to power" and standing up to the "powers and principalities." This group was formed after 9/11/01 by some of L.A.'s major religious leaders in order to promote peace with justice. Besides organizing educational events, vigils, and demonstrations, we have stood in solidarity with the Muslim community when it has come under attack. Since becoming involved with ICUJP, I have visited a Muslim imam named Abdul Jabbar Hamdan who was arrested on trumped-up charges and held in detention for over two years. Ironically, in front of the detention center where this man was held, there is a statue in memory of the Japanese Americans who were unjustly detained during World War II. By visiting Hamdan, I feel that I am following in the footsteps of Quakers who visited the Japanese internees then. Hamdan was finally released in the summer of 2006 because of lack of evidence, but the U.S. government is still seeking to deport him to Jordan, which he left 25 years ago, and where he could be subject to imprisonment and torture.

I believe that we are called as Friends to support the prophetic work of interfaith organizations such ICUJP, Tikkun, and the Shalom Center of Philadelphia. It is crucially important for Friends to join in the work of these "spiritual progressives."

Grounds for Hope

Interfaith work is not only important, it is also an incredibly joyful experience. When Muslims, Jews, Christians, and others come together to worship and to work on common concerns, there is often a sense of joy and mutual appreciation too deep for words. Many of these gatherings are celebratory, with music, ethnic food, dance, and various worship experiences. Youth and community leaders are honored. Stimulating panel discussions take place and one's spiritual horizons are broadened. For those who haven't experienced such gatherings, I recommend either going to one and/or watching the video *God and Allah Need to Talk* by

Ruth Broyde Sharone. Whatever the format of interfaith gatherings, people come away uplifted; and I sense the Divine Presence at work.

These gatherings also offer grounds for hope. I see parallels between the rise of the interfaith movement and the "citizen diplomacy" movement of the 1980s that helped to end the Cold War. Reaching out to the Russians during the Reagan era was my first Quaker concern. It still warms my heart to think back on this Spirit-led work, which I described in a Pendle Hill pamphlet, *Spiritual Linkage with Russians: the Story of a Leading*. Although conservatives believe that the Cold War ended because Ronald Reagan put so much pressure on the Russians that they finally gave up and cried "uncle," there is considerable evidence that "people power" and citizen diplomacy helped to convince both Reagan and Gorbechev that the time was ripe for ending the Cold War. This trust-building movement didn't accomplish miracles overnight, however. It began rather modestly in the 1950s when small delegations went to the Soviet Union to begin a dialogue and create friendship.

A similar process of trust-building in the Middle East began in the 1980s and 1990s with groups like American Friends Service Committee and Fellowship of Reconciliation leading delegations and teaching listening skills. In 2004 I went to Israel/Palestine with another trust-building group, the Compassionate Listening Project. Our delegation of Christians, Jews, Muslims, and Buddhists stayed at a kibbutz, a refugee camp, Christian retreat centers, and a school in Bethlehem. We conversed with those in the Israeli/Palestinian peace movement as well as with settlers. One of the most heart-wrenching experiences was listening as parents shared with us the pain of losing their children in the recent violence. I will never forget the Palestinian family who told us how their 16-year-old son, a peace activist, was shot in the head by Israeli police in front of his mother, nor will I forget the rabbi who has dedicated his life to helping families heal from such trauma after his son was murdered by Palestinians. I will also carry the memory of an elderly Jewish man named Steve who invited a young Palestinian named Asmi into his home in Jerusalem and treated him like a son. Steve became the guest of honor at Asmi's wedding and is now part of his loving Palestinian family.

These encounters help us understand the human depths and complexities of today's conflicts. Despite war and terrorism, trust-building work has expanded since 9/11/01 and now includes mainstream groups such as the Rotary Club International. This reconciliation work goes largely unreported in the media, which tends to focus on the sensational. However, I am convinced that these efforts on the part of ordinary people will have an enormous impact over the long run, and that we are called to do this work as Friends.

William Penn and Tom Fox

As Friends respond to the call of the interfaith movement, we do well to keep in mind two Friends whose examples speak powerfully to our times. One speaks primarily to the head, the other to the heart.

William Penn was one of the great intellectual as well as religious figures of colonial America. Growing up in an age of religious war and conflict, and raised in a military family, Penn was utterly transformed by the experience of Quakerism. He renounced violence. He came to believe that the Light of God is present in all human beings, and in all religions. He founded the Quaker colony of Pennsylvania as a place where people of all faiths could practice their religions without government interference—a revolutionary idea at the time. Penn's willingness to allow freedom of religion in Pennsylvania had a significant impact on our country's commitment to religious pluralism. Furthermore, Penn envisioned a world in which nations would settle their disputes by law, not war. In 1693, he wrote a plan, *An Essay Towards the Present and Future Peace of Europe*, which is considered a prototype of the United Nations.

I believe that as Friends, we are called upon to carry forward the legacy of Penn and to work diligently for a society based on tolerance and a world governed by international law. We are called to support the Quaker United Nations Office and other efforts to strengthen the UN, especially since many in the religious right in our country equate the UN with the Antichrist. We need to share our view with others in our country that the United Nations, despite all its flaws, still offers the best hope we have for a peaceful and just world.

Another Friend whose example calls to us and to our time is Tom Fox, who was taken hostage and then killed in Iraq last year. No Friend is better known throughout the world today, especially in the Muslim world. Tom Fox speaks to the heart of our Quaker faith. Like Mary Dyer, Mary Fisher, and other early Friends who were called to travel in the ministry, he was willing to risk his life to bear witness to the power of love and the

Inward Light. He was also part of the interfaith movement; although he considered himself a Christian, he was open to spiritual insights from other religions, such as Buddhism, Judaism, and Islam. He went to Israel/Palestine and listened to all sides in this tragic conflict. He lived side-by-side with the Iraqi people ánd took up their cause and their concerns. He showed by his example what it means, in George Fox's words, to "walk cheerfully over the world, answering that of God in every one."

When news of Tom Fox's death was announced, he was deeply mourned by the Muslim community, which will always remember and honor him. A young Muslim man I know, Yasir Shah, wrote a letter to *Friends Bulletin*: "I'm heartbroken to say that it's only recently that I've come to find out about such a courageous and dedicated man...I believe that Tom Fox's family, the American people, and the Iraqi people were blessed to have someone of his caliber to fight for them...Tom Fox embodied the characteristics of the leaders of the Civil Rights Movement...[and] I pray that we increase our unity in the stand against injustice, and continue to strive for the rights of all humans."

Not all of us, certainly, have the calling or the courage to follow Tom Fox's example. But we are called to honor his memory and to carry forward his spirit as best we can in our Quaker witness to the world.

November 15, 1983

Scattering Seeds in International Peace Work

by Joe Peacock

T he first thing to understand about international peace work is that it can be very lonely. Some moments are exciting, of course, but there are long, lonely spaces in between. International peace work involves leaving your family and friends and living in a place where you do not speak the language and may not have the occasion to do so since you are not directly involved with the people there. It means spending a lot of time behind a typewriter, writing to friends and colleagues in other countries or writing articles for magazines and not knowing if anyone reads them; it means collecting information about peace movements in different parts of the world and wondering whether you should be out there yourself. It often means having the impression of scattering seeds and not being able to wait to see whether they sprout.

In 1981, I came to work at IFOR through the Brethren Volunteer Service in the United States. I was excited about coming to the Netherlands, where I had never been, but adjusting to the move was difficult, especially in the first months. It felt strange: too small, too flat, too tidy, and perhaps even too affluent. People seemed very self-sufficient and difficult to get to know. I felt a little like I was living in a dollhouse; I could look into people's big windows but not go inside. Most difficult of all was living in a country where I did not speak the language. No matter how well people can speak English, I do not feel right in a place until I can speak the local language. A tree is just not the same as a *boom* and never will be. My feeling of isolation was increased because I was living alone for the first time. So one aspect of my experience of international peace work has been learning to live here in Alkmaar, struggling with Dutch and trying to get to know the local people.

Another, larger aspect is the reason I am here: to work for peace. I was very impressed with the size, the spirit, and the sophistication of the Dutch peace movement. I saw here, even more clearly than in the United States, the importance of moving beyond making "calls" for peace—which Quakers have made so often in their history—to building a broad based campaign with political strength on positions such as unilateral initiatives ("Rid the World of Nuclear Weapons, Beginning with the Netherlands") or a bilateral freeze of nuclear weapons. As I observed peace movements with political strength, such as The Dutch Inter-church Peace Council (1KV) and The Campaign for Nuclear Disarmament, and political parties with peace convictions, such as the Progressive Socialist Party (PSP) and Die Grünen, I realized more clearly the importance of not being afraid of the compromises and power struggles of the political world.

But I slowly began to realize that while political campaigns are essential in moving us toward disarmament, peace involves much more than the conducting of such campaigns: peace involves not only the minds but also and especially the *hearts* and the *consciences* of people. I came to understand that there is, in fact, a clearly religious element in this struggle, for nonbelievers and believers alike. Peace is a question, after all, not only of our ideas but of our commitments. It is something that reaches to our souls and calls us to conversion. Perhaps it was the same insight that was recently given expression by an American professor, Robert Holmes, who wrote, "The problem isn't so much a lack of desire for peace as it is a commitment to institutions (such as the military and military related industry) that make peace impossible."

I had come to work at IFOR with the idea that our highest priority should be to work for disarmament, but eventually I realized that the real task was something deeper, something involving our deepest commitments and motivations. So while I had not thought much about nonviolence before coming here, I realized that this deepening of perspective offered by nonviolence and the commitment to nonviolence as "truth force" are most central to the struggle for peace. There were many influences which moved my thinking in this direction. One was Creuza Macid, a former Brazilian nun who worked for a year in the IFOR office making European contacts for *Servicio Paz y Justicia*, the nonviolence movement in Latin America. Creuza had absolute faith in the strength of nonviolence even in the midst of the violence and injustice she had experienced in the barrios of São Paulo. She was lonely so far from her friends and in such a different culture. But one could easily see that her commitment was a fire that could not be extinguished.

Peace camps are another continuing influence, especially the women's peace camps like those at Greenham Common and Soesterberg. The total commitment by the women who make a permanent form of protest of this kind offers a witness to the urgency of the present situation and to the ability of ordinary people to do something about it.

The one person who moved my thinking most decisively in the direction of nonviolence was Jean Goss, a former French trade unionist who became a pacifist when he was a prisoner of war in World War II. With his wife, Hildegard Goss Mayr, Jean has traveled and evangelized the gospel of nonviolence from Brazil to Poland. Both are still traveling extensively for IFOR and co-serving as IFOR's vice presidents.

I first met Jean during an IFOR executive committee meeting, when he took a group of us aside for a "discussion" which turned out to be a half hour lecture on nonviolence. He told the story of peasants in Latin America who had undertaken a nonviolent struggle to obtain water for their village by reaching the consciences of those in power. He told of trade unionists who lay down in front of the trucks driven by strikebreakers because they had nothing in their lives to lose, and who eventually succeeded in reaching the consciences of their opponents. He said that we in the peace movement must not be satisfied with sitting in an office collecting and distributing information; we must aggressively *attack* the base of public support for nuclear weapons and not be afraid of using our reason and conviction in confronting with the truth those in power. By the end of his talk I was holding back tears because in this man I had personally experienced the power of the truth. I knew that I was in the presence of one like George Fox, who knew that the spiritual war in which we are engaged—the Lamb's war—must be aggressively fought with the spiritual weapons at our disposal.

This kind of understanding of the true nature of the struggle for peace has helped me understand what I already knew: that the important aspects of my work, as of the rest of my life, are not the ideas or the discussions, but the *experiences* I share with individuals, the glimpses of these deeper commitments on the part of those around me. These are people like Drummond Petrie, a Quaker cellist who left a job with the Rome opera to devote himself to music therapy and peace work, and Anna Luisa L'Abbate, who left a husband and grown children in Florence to help found a peace camp in Sicily, and Anita Kromberg, who had worked with those seeking a violent overthrow of the apartheid regime in South Africa until a voice inside told her there must be another way and she discovered a small community of other individuals working for nonviolent change there.

These "high" experiences have not always focused on other people, but have sometimes consisted of things I have done myself, moments when my actions seemed particularly "right." I will never forget a day at the peace camp in Comiso in Sicily. In the center of Comiso stands a monument commemorating various occasions of popular resistance. One large stone proclaims "La Resistenza Continua," while others are devoted to particular resisters such as Ché Guevara or Martin Luther King, Jr. On this afternoon a group of us decided to clean the monument, which had become littered with dirt and trash. It was a quiet way of saying that we wanted to bring out of the dust a noble tradition of resistance and establish it there in Comiso, where U.S. cruise missiles are to be installed.

That evening a public meeting was held at the monument to discuss resistance to the missiles, and a big question was violence versus nonviolence. Many of those present had hardly heard of nonviolence before. I was asked to speak and explained that I was one American who had come here to see to it that a lot of other Americans would not come to Comiso. I explained that 1,700 Americans had been arrested in New York for making a successful nonviolent blockade of the five nuclear powers' missions to the U.N. during the Special Session. The reaction to my talk was quite good. Perhaps, I thought, those dead stones could bring to life real resistance once again, and I was pleased that I was part of it.

Easter at Molesworth peace camp in England offered another such occasion. I helped two friends convert a bit of the future cruise missile base into a garden of vegetables, trees, and flowers. The action was itself part of a wedding of two young Quakers, with the "official" part taking place at the Leicester Meetinghouse on Saturday, and the concluding worship held at the peace camp on Sunday, followed by the planting. It made me reflect on our covenant responsibilities not only to our husbands and wives but to our world, and on the resistance that is undertaken by a single seed as it struggles against the darkness and the cold and the pressure of the earth in its climb to the light. But best of all was simply standing around the campfire in the cold on Saturday night, singing together and falling into a spontaneous and rich silence. The pleasantly hard physical work of life at the peace camp balanced my office existence.

Sometimes I find it hard to return to Alkmaar after such experiences—back to the perpetual rain, the perpetual mail to be answered, the perpetual flood of peace movement publications and regular press which cannot possibly all be read. The overwhelming flow of information and the time that must be spent on infinite small tasks is the most trying aspect of this work. Days and weeks pass in which I sense I'm not getting anything accomplished.

The next most trying feature of international peace work is conferences. I have lost count of the number of conferences I have attended since I have been here, but it must be getting close to ten. Each time I am convinced that this one should be the last. Inevitably the workshops are too large or the discussion is too brief or the reports are boring or the final document is useless. I am convinced that the peace movement puts too much time, energy, and money into conferences, which generally are a poor structure for people to communicate well. But just as inevitable as the problems are the exceptions: good discussions, exciting reports, the old friends I am happy to see again. And so I continue going to conferences and struggling through them.

Occasionally, conferences give me brief glimpses of the Kingdom, which keeps me going through the dry times. Less than a week ago, for example, I was sharing a cool, breezy evening with a friend, Greger Hatt of the Swedish FOR. We were sitting on the Charles Bridge in Prague, having just left the closing reception of the Peace Assembly which we had attended for our organizations. Before us was the illuminated castle, where the last lingerers at the reception were starting to make their way home, and beyond the castle rose the Gothic spires of the Cathedral of St. Vitus. Behind us was a full moon, which reflected from the ripple of the Vltava River below. All around us were the saints that line the sides of the 14th-century bridge.

At that moment there was no place in the world we would rather have been than sitting on that bridge, though we knew that some hundreds of kilometers to the east and the west two great military powers were maintaining their endless watch in preparation for the unleashing of the powers of death. Leaning against the wall of the old bridge, we wondered whether the conference had moved the world any further from the abyss, and whether we had made a mark on this gathering of 3,000. Had our talk about nonviolence been heard—could it be heard by those participants who had come from liberation struggles in various parts of the Third World? Had our tactful, respectful attitude toward the representatives of the official Peace Councils in the East been untrue to the more prophetic challenge of speaking against injustice wherever we find it? And why is our nonviolent movement so small? Why are we a minority at any gathering of the peace movement, East or West?

Though we seldom see the results of what we do, we simply must continue scattering seeds in the hope that some will come up. In the meantime, we are gifted with more than enough evenings like that one, the small glimpses of the Kingdom and of communion with fellow workers for peace to make the difficult times worthwhile.

Seeking Peace in Prisons

P rison witness has been practiced in Great Britain since the beginning of the Religious Society of Friends. It may, therefore, be appropriate to begin this section with an in-depth article by an English Quaker concerning the witness he and many other Friends have been doing with prisoners on death row in the United States today. One hundred and thirty-seven countries have no death penalty, while thirty-seven do. The United States is in the latter group. In the United States, twelve states have no death penalty; thirty-eight do. The number of persons, mostly but not all men, on death row in any one state ranges from one to almost 700 (July 2009 figures). Most are some shade of brown and many are involved in long, drawn-out appeals. In the past few years, numerous prisoners have been exonerated with new evidence and set free, usually with a few dollars and little to no support to help them to readjust to a much changed world from the one they left many years before. Restitution and support differ by state. Many Friends are engaged in attempts to abolish the death penalty and at the same time to make justice and release a more fair and rehabilitative process. Some Friends' meetings have prison worship groups under their care. Insiders and outsiders who participate cherish these meetings.

The largest single program of prison work by Friends in the United States today is probably the Alternatives to Violence Program. In Robert Dockhorn's interview with Steve Angell, readers can learn about AVP's inception, growth, and major focus: "transformative power." In listening to Steve's voice, readers can also sense the spiritual depth of the Friends who took AVP through its beginnings. You will recall in the section on peace in the home and school that AVP is the program that Fenna Mandolang, a junior high Friend, brought to her school. Fenna was inspired by the spiritual depth of the adult Friends with whom she interned in AVP, including Steve Angell. The next article is the testimony of a prisoner who has gone through AVP workshops. His reflections echo those of many others. Not represented here are the many AVP workshops that have been held in communities, First-day schools, and yearly meetings.

S.H.

December 1996

Light on Death Row:
FRIENDS JOURNAL Cadbury Event,
July 4, 1996, Hamilton, Ontario

by Jan Arriens

One evening in November 1987, I had nothing in particular to do and idly switched on the television. It was a program about a young African American executed in Mississippi, which I had earlier decided not to watch, as I thought it would be altogether too depressing.

Within minutes I was riveted. *Fourteen Days in May* remains the most compelling television documentary I have ever seen. For reasons that remain obscure, the BBC was permitted to take its cameras into the maximum security unit of Parchman Penitentiary in Mississippi in May 1987 and film the last 14 days in the life of Edward Earl Johnson.

As the documentary proceeded, the viewer felt a terrible sense of impotence at what was happening, which was so manifestly wrong—whatever one's views on the death penalty. Edward Earl Johnson radiated a very special quality: a quiet charm, honesty, and simplicity. Guards, the chaplain, the attorneys—all expressed their liking for Edward Earl and clearly did not want the execution to proceed.

The voice of humanity, however, came from the least expected quarter: the other prisoners. Three other prisoners were interviewed in the film. The words of one, in particular, affected me profoundly. At ten past ten in the evening, less than two hours before the scheduled execution, one of the prisoners said quietly but with great feeling: "Everyone here is dying tonight, a part of them. I can never be the same after this. We're supposed to be vicious and cruel, but this goes beyond anything that anyone could ever do."

My overwhelming reaction was one of astonishment that a prisoner should have been able to say exactly what I was feeling, but was unable to express. I remember breaking down at that point.

I wrote to all three prisoners. All three replied. The first to do so was a man called Leo Edwards. I had never received a letter that had moved me more. He had been on death row for six years. His letter ended with the words, "May God be between you and harm and all the empty places you walk." How could someone in the bleakest and darkest of situations worry about the "empty places" in which I walked?

Shortly afterwards, I received a letter from a man called Sam Johnson. It turned out to be Sam who had spoken the words that had affected me so much. He wrote that he was from Rochester, N.Y., that he had been on death row for six years, and that he was innocent. "I haven't seen any of my family since I've been here, and I never knew that loneliness could hurt so very much. I don't mean to cry upon your shoulder but speaking about this place one can find very little that's happy to speak about."

The letters were very far removed from my stereotype picture of death row prisoners as subhuman monsters. Here were people reaching out and displaying compassion, sensitivity, and insight. I showed the letters to others, who also began writing. My local meeting organized that most English of events, a cream tea in a village garden, and publicity of this curious event in the local Cambridge newspaper attracted about 30 correspondents. Through this we also learned that the brilliant young English death row lawyer who had represented Edward Earl, Clive Stafford Smith, then based in Atlanta, came from near Cambridge, and I met him that summer.

I also got in touch with Amnesty International, who were highly enthusiastic and supportive.

Later in 1988, the Quaker weekly *The Friend* published excerpts from Sam's letters. In one letter he wrote: "In spite of all this I still believe in mankind. These people and this experience have taken me so low that I have to 'reach up' to touch bottom, but I still believe in mankind."

In another he wrote:

> For the first year or so I was filled to the brim with pure hatred over what had happened to me. Losing all I had and everyone I loved filled me so full of hatred I almost did go crazy. All of it drained out of me when it dawned upon me that I had to stop thinking about all I had lost and start thinking about what I could gain, even from the worst of positions a person could be in.

As a result of this publicity, about 30 Quakers throughout Britain began writing as well. LifeLines had been born.

What we rapidly discovered was not only that the men displayed qualities we had not expected to encounter on death row, but that they almost invariably told the same story. They were all poor. All had received bad legal representation. Many were African American. The vast majority came from broken homes and had suffered from violence and sexual abuse in childhood. Their parents were often alcoholics. Many had little education, had gotten hooked on drugs in their teens, and ended up on death row in early adulthood. Some had been juveniles at the time of the crime. It became apparent to us just how easy it was to end up on death row in the United States. While there are deeply disturbed men and women on death row, there are also many essentially "normal" people of whom we can truly say, "There but for the grace of God go I."

Their backgrounds were really brought home to me in late 1988, when I went to the United States to meet Sam and the others. Leo Edwards told me that he thanked God for being on death row. I asked him what on earth he could mean. He explained that death row had been the first period of real stability in his life. In his words, it had given him an appreciation of love and of life that he had never had before. Sam Johnson told me that in comparison with his classmates, his lot was a fortunate one, as most had either met violent deaths or were drug addicts on the streets of New York.

The way in which the death penalty in the United States punishes life's losers was graphically brought out by a Californian death row attorney, Jay Pultz, who spoke at a LifeLines conference in 1994. Jay said that one of his clients had told him he was one of six boys from the same urban kindergarten class who had all ended up on death row. We are, surely, dealing here not with individual criminal pathology but with a social phenomenon. Here, it seems to me, U.S. society is like a boiling cauldron. The death penalty is an attempt to keep the lid on the cauldron, whereas what needs to be done is to douse the fires—the fires of broken families, drug abuse, and lack of gun control.

We also discovered the extraordinary lengths of time that people spend on death row. One of the original three I wrote to, John Irving, was sentenced to death at the age of 20. When I met him, he had been there for 12 years. His death sentence was overturned last year, at the age of 39. He had spent his entire adult life—and half his total life—on death row.

Many of the men are abandoned and rejected by their families and friends. This is why the correspondence can be so important to them. Last April I met a man, John Nixon, aged 68, whom I had also spoken to in 1988. In the intervening seven years, he had not had another personal visitor. A man of 27 whom I met in 1988 had not had a personal visitor in all the four years he had been on death row.

I know that many of you know a great deal about death row, but others of you may not, and it may be as well to outline the overall situation. There are at present a little over 3,000 men and 49 women on death row in the United States. A number have been there since the death penalty was reintroduced in 1976. Until recently, a map of the United States shading in the executing states was virtually a map of the Confederacy in the Civil War, with the five main executing states being Texas, Florida, Virginia, Louisiana, and Georgia. Illinois has now also become a major executing state.

Since 1976 there have been about 330 executions, and nearly 1,500 convictions or sentences have been reversed. What these figures mean is that out of a total of a little over 4,700 people who have entered the portals of death row since 1976, just under 7 percent have been executed and in a little over 30 percent of cases the state is saying, "We got it wrong. You should never have been there in the first place." This figure of 30 percent can only rise, as more men have their sentences or convictions overturned after many years in the appeals process.

The system of nine different courts that prisoners can go through is designed to ensure the ultimate certainty for the ultimate punishment. But mistakes are still made. What it shows above all is that the death penalty cannot be both just and humane: rush it through and innocent people will die, try to be just and it becomes a hideous, protracted cat-and-mouse game. This to me is one of the biggest arguments against the death penalty, although it is not often made. The death penalty is also about the way that society deals with those most at its mercy. It is essentially about revenge and retribution and provides no room for compassion, remorse, or change.

A few words about LifeLines. In all we have probably put the best part of 5,000 people in Britain and Ireland in touch with prisoners on death row. We also have members in a large number of European countries and in Australia. In 1991 I put together a book of extracts from the prisoners' letters, entitled *Welcome To Hell*. A few months later, in early 1992, the BBC screened a film based on one of the chapters in this book, about the correspondence between a retired music teacher in England, Mary Grayson, and Ray Clark in Florida during the last few months of his life. In response I received an astonishing 6,500 letters from people wanting to write. By no means all joined, but it was in that year that the organization really took off. I am glad to say that *Welcome to Hell* is being republished early next year in the United States, by Northeastern University Press in Boston, Mass. Many people have told me that *Welcome to Hell* is one of the most powerful and moving books they have ever read. A number of British prisoners are even writing to death row inmates as a result of the book.

LifeLines has a quarterly newsletter, and we hold two conferences each year, for which we fly out speakers from the United States. Speakers have included Clive Stafford Smith and Sister Helen Prejean, before she wrote her book *Dead Man Walking*. We have regional groups and "coordinators" for each of the states, who provide a vital link between the correspondents and the prisoners. Right from the outset we decided that we should be nonpolitical and not campaign. We also have a team of voluntary counselors to help a LifeLiner when the prisoner he or she is writing to faces execution and to deal with the problems that come up in the correspondence.

At present, LifeLines has around 1,500 members, but the total number of people writing is much greater—probably around 3,000—as people join, start writing, and then drop out of the organization. For several years now, we have been able to say that every prisoner on death row wanting a pen pal has been given one. Many write to more than one person. For some prisoners, in fact, the correspondence has become an almost full-time office job. Most of us writing to them feel that the prisoners have given us as much or more than we have given them. To share with someone under such a terrible threat—no matter what they have done—is to be given an extraordinary glimpse into the triumph of the human spirit in adversity. We have also found the correspondence to be far more equal and two-way than we had ever imagined. Several hundred letter-writers have now gone to the United States to visit the person they got to know so well on paper.

What can the correspondence mean to the prisoner? An African

American man whom I met in Georgia writes to a much older woman in a small town near where I live in England. Johnny once wrote to her:

You know I never thought I could ever care about a person or truly trust anyone again in my life. You showed me wrong because I can be with you totally, I'm not afraid to express my hurts to you or my fear, nor afraid to tell you who I am. That alone means so much to me when I had closed myself up from everyone, keeping the door to self locked up, I don't have to place masks over the face of my real self.

Last year I attended a clemency hearing in Louisiana held on Maundy Thursday. The prisoner, Antonio James, was facing his 13th death date. During a recess, I was introduced to him by Sister Helen Prejean. Antonio faced execution four days later, and this poorly educated man was, quite literally, pleading for his life. Despite the enormous stress he was under, he reached out his manacled hand and, with tears in his eyes, said that "the love and support I received from two English ladies I didn't know before was one of the most beautiful things that ever happened in my life."

Antonio James was unexpectedly reprieved, but was executed in March this year.

But there are also other problems in the correspondence. The main ones are money and sex. Nearly all the prisoners are male and most of the British correspondents—85 percent—are female. The combination of needy, intensely deprived, men and compassionate women is obviously a potentially explosive one. Difficulties in forming relationships with the opposite sex are often an integral part of the prisoners' stories, and they may feel they have to "come on strong" in order to prove themselves. One woman wrote back that there was no need for the prisoner to do this, but that she accepted him as he was. He wrote back saying that no woman had ever said this to him before. Time and again, women have found that if they can hold firm at this point, the two can then work through distorted and unrealistic romantic feelings and fantasies to reach the clearer waters of genuine friendship: something many of the men say they have never experienced before, and which they come to regard as one of the most valuable things in their lives.

Sometimes the problems are unexpected. One woman recently wrote to a man in Texas on some new primrose notepaper she had bought. She said she was using it as it cheered her up and gave her a lift.

The prisoner took this to be a coded message that the paper was impregnated with drugs and wrote back complaining: "I have eaten all four pages of your letter, but I don't feel any different."

But what, you may ask, about the victims and their families? Are we concentrating on the wrong people?

I remember a woman in Ireland who was writing to a prisoner, also in Georgia, who was deeply troubled by what he had done and asked her whether he should write to the victim's parents for forgiveness. He wished to do so, but was held back by the fear of rejection, which had been such a big theme in his life. Slowly and prayerfully, she—an Irish Catholic—persuaded her Southern Baptist friend to take the risk. He wrote. By return he received a letter saying that the parents understood and forgave him.

Within LifeLines, one of our members, Lesley Moreland, a Quaker, asked if she could write to a prisoner on death row after her own 23-year-old daughter, Ruth, had been murdered. Lesley came to a crossroads in her life. She decided to write to someone on death row as she felt the need to hold on to the difference between the act of murder and the whole person. The man in Texas she wrote to happened to have lost his own mother in a murder; Lesley has been to Texas to meet him and his family. She also met the victim's family there. In 1995, after years of discrete and patient negotiation, Lesley managed to visit in prison the young man who had murdered her daughter.

Equally as remarkable is the story of another LifeLines member, Leanne, who as a child of 13 was raped, stabbed, beaten with a brick, and left for dead. But to this day she feels forgiveness and hopes that her attacker has overcome his anger—although she knows that he has gone on to rape again. She writes,

> The physical torture or death of this boy would not help me in any way. Would this family's suffering ease my own family's suffering? No. There would be no "balancing" the scales. It would only have created more victims, more suffering, more heartache. As an 'almost victim' I give the death penalty the definite thumbs down.

Leanne, too, is writing to a prisoner under sentence of death.

These two members of our organization both spoke at our 1994 conference held in Edinburgh. Other speakers included Pat Bane, the chairperson of the U.S. organization Murder Victims' Families for Reconciliation, and Betty Foster, the mother of a juvenile offender executed in Georgia in 1992. She, too, was a victim.

I have often wondered what it is about death row that can affect those of us writing to the condemned men so deeply. Part of this is because it touches the depths of the human psyche. As I see it, we all live in three kinds of prison. First of all, there is the physical prison of our particular circumstances—the country and house we live in, our bodies, and our physical limitations. Secondly, there is the emotional prison of our minds and personalities. Thirdly, we are in a spiritual prison, in the sense of living in the mystery, or as Paul put it, seeing through a glass darkly. We may have a sense of inner awareness, or a sense of presence, and occasionally people have transcendent experiences that change their lives. But for the most part the intimations of another dimension of consciousness are subtle, tantalizing, and elusive.

Now prisoners are, of course, very obviously in physical confinement: on death row they spend 23 hours a day in a steel and concrete cage. In terms of the second category, our psychological imprisonment, prison is also a deeply traumatizing experience, in which many of the weaknesses, fears, and pains that put people there in the first place are made far worse. In these circumstances, it is to me deeply inspiring to find prisoners who retain and indeed develop their humanity and inner spiritual resources, seemingly against all the odds, in this human hell.

I remember that when I met the 12 prisoners on death row in Mississippi and Georgia in 1988, it was very evident—sometimes painfully, sometimes uplifting—how the men were thrust back on their own resources in the solitude and deprivation of their cells. Some were all but broken by the experience, but others had risen above it. Nothing summed it up better than the words of Willie Reddix in Mississippi: "Sometimes you can be so still you can hear the grass grow. Sometimes you can be so still you can hear the voices of the children who must once have played even in fields like these." Another prisoner spoke of the peace of mind he had developed in prison, calling it the "quiet light."

When I met Leo Edwards in 1988, it was just three months after he came within 12 hours of execution. He heard on the radio that he had been given a stay. He had given up hope. Talking to this poorly educated man who had looked death in the face was an experience I shall never forget. He told me that he had made his peace, and that death no longer held any fear for him. Eight months later he was dead.

Sam Johnson wrote to me that he sometimes thinks of life as an hourglass, with each moment being a grain of sand. Perhaps when we die the hourglass is turned over and all the sand runs through again without our being able to change it.

> I don't really know if life is as I've tried to describe it or not, but, if it is, and if I love all that I can this day, if I laugh all that I can this day, if I give all of the happiness that I can this day, if I do the least amount of bad that I can this day, then when this day comes back to me I won't want to change it even if I could.

Some years ago, my meeting in Cambridge "adopted" Sam: we even obtained special dispensation from London Yearly Meeting, and he is an Associate Member of Hartington Grove Meeting: the only Friend in the world, as far as I know, with that status! In late 1992 I attended Sam's resentencing trial in Vicksburg, Va., and am glad to say that he had his sentence overturned and is off death row.

In the last few months, another man I write to, Mike Lambrix in Florida, has come very close to the end of his appeals. He has been on death row for 13 years, and is now aged 36. By his own confession he arrived on death row as an alcoholic and a drifter. A few months ago, Mike wrote to me that he was nearly executed in 1988. He writes:

> The morning of the scheduled execution I woke up literally in a cold sweat. It was more than just a nightmare; it was an "out of body" experience. I didn't just dream it, I physically felt it, even the execution. And awoke just as the bright light consumed everything. The immense light I sensed as I was awaking was not a physical, environmental light, as that obviously would have been noticed by the guards who stood watch over me. This light I can only describe as that sense of light people experiencing "near death" experiences describe.

He goes on to say that this was the day when God died for him and when he lost the sense of presence he had always had before.

> And although that may sound as if I deny God—I do not. Rather, it's my belief that God is the collective consciousness, that eternal inner-self.
>
> I must admit that there are times since the "death" of that former perception of God when I really miss that "personal" feeling. The way this transformation of my spirituality came about, it allows me to relate to the anguish Jesus felt at the moment of his death—how he cried out "why hast thou forsaken me," as I think that he too felt that absence

and emptiness of the spiritual inner-self. Yet equally so, I truly believe that I did not actually lose anything, but I gained a new and "more enlightened" perspective of what this thing we call "God" is, and more importantly, whereas before I could only wonder if there was life after "death," I am now unequivocally convinced that not only is there "life" after mortal death, but that we "lived" before this mortal existence. Our "personal" God is a reflection of our spiritual selfishness, and as long as we want to possess it, then we are limited in our growth and perception of collectiveness.

I think these words have much to say to us Quakers. I am anguished that Mike, who is right at the end of his appeals, may be dead in three months. [Mike Lambrix lost his appeal in the Florida Supreme Court in September.-Eds.] Mike is not representative of the men and women on death row, but, as we have seen with Sam Johnson, nor is he unique. There are many, many men who, in their long years of incarceration under threat of death, have grown enormously in the Spirit.

This meeting point between imprisonment and the spiritual life is integral to our Quaker experience. At the very start of his ministry, Fox had his famous vision in which "I saw also that there was an ocean of darkness and death, but an infinite ocean of light and love, which flowed over the ocean of darkness." What we often tend to overlook is the preceding passage, in which Fox writes of being shown all sorts of depravities by the Lord. "Why should I be thus, seeing I was never addicted to commit these evils?" he cries. "And the Lord answered that it was needful I should have a sense of all conditions how else should I speak to all conditions: and in this I saw the infinite love of God."

Prisons and imprisonment are deeply burned into the Quaker consciousness. Some estimate that as many as one in five Quakers were imprisoned for their beliefs in the early days, and George Fox's *Journal* is of course full of his experiences in prisons.

In the United States, as you know far better than I do, early Quakers were persecuted by the Puritans in the Massachusetts Bay Colony, and four Quakers were executed around 1660: the Boston Common martyrs.

In 1959, marking the tercentenary of those events, Henry Cadbury wrote in FRIENDS JOURNAL, "The best memorial is doubtless the recognition of the principles for which men [sic] died and the practice of them in our life today."

William Penn rejected "the wickedness of exterminating, where it was possible to reform," and Pennsylvania set a lead in the abolition of the death penalty. In Britain, Elizabeth Fry's work visiting women prisoners carried forward the Quaker tradition of penal reform. She and others also worked steadfastly for abolition. In the long and often shameful history of capital punishment in Britain, Harry Potter has written: "One Christian group alone stands out: at every turn, running every society, campaigning everywhere, were the Quakers. They alone, as a Christian body, were completely and absolutely opposed to the death penalty." The death penalty was abolished in Britain 30 years ago, and in Canada 20 years ago, while it is just over 20 years since it was reintroduced in the United States.

Which brings me to the situation in the United States. Here I feel I must tread with great caution. It is not for me to come barging in with insensitive suggestions and criticism. I can only speak to you out of our experience in LifeLines and from the Quaker tradition.

Some U.S. Friends have told me that the Quaker response to the death penalty has been oddly muted. But there have been enormously encouraging developments among Quakers of late. The Friends Committee to Abolish the Death Penalty (FCADP) was set up in 1993. Recently, hundreds of Quaker activists for the FCADP handed out literature at cinemas where *Dead Man Walking* was showing. Friends helped collect the 20,000 signatures to abolish the death penalty that were delivered to President Clinton—a magnificent and inspiring achievement—to mark the 20th anniversary of the reinstatement of the death penalty. Several yearly meetings have adopted minutes reaffirming their opposition to capital punishment.

What lessons have we learned in LifeLines, and what can we impart to you?

In the first place, by being deliberately nonpolitical, we have, I believe, paradoxically achieved far more than had we set out to campaign. This is because we have focused on the human face of death row. People have asked to write because, like the rest of us, they have been impressed by the human qualities they have seen or read about, qualities they had not expected to encounter on death row. In your campaigning, I think you will be far more effective if you focus on individual human beings and bring their stories to the attention of the public. One case that people can relate to no matter what the man may have done—can get through to people in a way that no learned arguments or statistics ever can.

With this in mind, I am wondering whether individual meetings might "adopt" a prisoner. You could write to him, individually or as a meeting. You might even be able to visit him. You could, indeed you *should*, get in touch with his defense attorney before drawing public attention to his case. By getting to know him, he would become a real person, as we have discovered. This in turn would help in portraying him to the wider community as a human being—whatever his frailties. I have brought with me details on a number of prisoners who would dearly welcome such support.

Secondly, a plea: Many abolitionists are putting forward life without parole as an alternative to capital punishment. Despite the temptation, I hope you will not do so. To me, life without parole is a doctrine of despair and but one small rung up the moral ladder from the death penalty.

Finally, I wonder whether it might be possible for minutes to be adopted. The following text draws on the minute of Philadelphia Yearly Meeting:

> *We affirm our unwavering opposition to capital punishment, which has been a deeply felt testimony of Friends since the establishment of our Religious Society in the 17th century. Where the sanctity of human life has been violated, we must comfort those who have suffered, but not repeat that violation. True security lies in our reverence for human life and our recognition of the godliness in us all, whatever we may have done.*

I know that opposing the death penalty will not be easy for U.S. Friends, as the tide of public opinion is running so swiftly in the opposite direction. But I hope that you, supported by Friends elsewhere, such as in Canada and Britain, will do so. We owe this to our Quaker principles, to that Light within ourselves that recognizes that of God in every man and woman, no matter where they may be or what they may have done. And we owe it to our Quaker heritage, to the light still shining today of those who were imprisoned for their beliefs, to the light of those who died on Boston Common. We owe it to the light of those Friends who, down the centuries and in many countries, have done so much for the improvement of prison conditions and the abolition of the death penalty. And, dear Friends, most of all we owe it to the light cast by the Sam Johnsons and Mike Lambrixs of this world—a light sometimes like a giant beacon effortlessly crossing the Atlantic and sometimes flickering but never quite going out; a light shining from the darkest and most improbable of places.

What can you do?

You can get involved. There is no justice if everyone leaves the work of justice to everyone else. Here are several organizations working hard to abolish capital punishment. They need your help and support.

Friends Committee to Abolish the Death Penalty (now called Religious Organizing Against the Death Penalty Project)
c/o Ciminal Justice Program
American Friends Service Committee
1501 Cherry Street
Philadelphia, PA 19102
(215) 241-7130

National Coalition to Abolition the Death Penalty
1705 DeSales St., NW
Fifth Floor
Washington, DC 20036
(202) 331-4090

Amnesty International Program to Abolish the Death Penalty
5 Penn Plaza
New York, NY 10001
(212) 807-8400

Murder Victims' Families For Reconciliation
Beth Wood, Executive Director
2100 M St. NW
Suite 170-296
Washington, DC 20037
(877) 896-4702

October 2002

AVP: An Interview with Steve Angell

by Robert Dockhorn

Stephen L. Angell was an early participant and continues to be active in the Alternatives to Violence Project (AVP), a program that offers workshops on nonviolence in prisons and elsewhere. This interview took place in Kennett Square, Pa., on June 18, 2002.

How did you first become involved with AVP?

AVP started in New York Yearly Meeting. My first encounter with it came when AVP held its first workshop in 1975 at Greenhaven Prison. Lawrence Apsey, who was the founder of AVP, asked my wife and me to serve as hosts to one of the leaders, Bernard Lafayette, a right-hand man to Martin Luther King Jr. We happily agreed to have him in our home. Although I had no direct contact with that first workshop, we plied him with questions afterwards in the evenings. That workshop was quite different from the workshops that we conduct today. We had no manuals then. We just had the model of the Children's Creative Response to Conflict (CCRC) program, which started in New York Yearly Meeting about three years prior to AVP. The first workshop was very much centered on individuals telling stories of how they approached potentially violent situations with nonviolence.

So that was my first contact with the program. A number of years later, New York Yearly Meeting became a little concerned because the program was growing in size as an activity of the Peace and Social Action Committee. It was part of the Quaker Project on Community Conflict (QPCC)—not a very catchy name. The yearly meeting felt concerned lest the tail start wagging the dog because they had very little staff. AVP didn't exactly have staff, but it had a growing number of facilitators for the workshops and growing expenses. We were also trying to raise funds to support the program. It was decided to incorporate AVP as a separate organization, although it would still be under the sponsorship of the yearly meeting and would have a separate budget. The facilitators were at first going principally into Greenhaven and Auburn prisons, although prisoners throughout New York state were beginning to ask for workshops.

How long was it before you were actually leading workshops?

When they decided to incorporate and needed incorporators, Larry Apsey, a close friend of ours, asked me to be one, and I agreed; and then they needed a board of directors, so I agreed to serve on that. Larry Floyd was the first clerk of the board, and I succeeded him two or three years later when he died. So I was quickly drawn into the organization, and then my friends who were leading the workshops said, "Steve, you ought to know what we're doing; you should take a workshop." I didn't think I needed that; I'm not a person who walks around getting in fights, carrying a gun or a knife or a tool for protection. But I couldn't disagree with them. I said if I'm going to be supporting this program from the organizational side, maybe I should know what it's like. So I agreed to take a workshop with Larry Apsey in Fishkill Prison in New York. That was late 1980 or early 1981. And I learned something about myself in the workshop that led me to believe I was in the right place doing the right thing: I realized that there was violence in me, too. The way I responded verbally and the disagreements with my teenage children could be more or less violent depending on how I did it. From that point on, I feel that each workshop I participate in has had something to offer to me and that I have grown as a result.

I wonder if that's generally true of the leaders of AVP workshops—that they themselves benefit each time they lead?

I have come to realize that what has held volunteer AVP facilitators in the work is that they feel they are getting something out of it themselves. It is more than giving something to others, it is also getting something back. The demands for being a facilitator for an AVP workshop are considerable. Most of our workshops are weekend workshops, starting in the prisons on Friday, maybe Friday morning, and running through Sunday evening. That means giving up a lot of valuable personal time. And yet, individuals stay with it week after week and month after month.

At this time, you were a member of which meeting?
Bulls Head Meeting, in Purchase Quarterly Meeting of New York Yearly Meeting.

And Lawrence Apsey—what was his meeting?
Also Bulls Head. He and his wife, Virginia, had lived in New York City and were members of 15th Street Meeting. He had been the administrator of QPCC, a subcommittee of the Peace and Social Action Committee, which had various projects.

How did AVP get its name?
The name QPCC was a little awkward. Once, when the facilitating team was coming out of Greenhaven Prison in New York—a maximum security prison with the electric chair—the officer on the way out said, "How was your workshop in alternatives to violence?" We picked up on that. It is short and accurately describes what we are doing. It also gives an accurate impression about what the project's about because it was really by happenstance that we started in prisons. I've always seen the project as something that is much broader than just working with prisoners.

Who were some of the other individuals who were important in the early stages?
Lee Stern, Ellen Flanders, Janet Lugo, Mary Gray Legg, Ginny Floyd, Steve Stalonas, and Steve Levinsky come immediately to mind—got a lot of Steves involved here! There were many others.

Were key decisions made early that helped AVP grow so rapidly?
First of all, from the beginning we decided that this should be a volunteer project. In other words, we would not pay facilitators. Individuals would do it because they wanted to, and that was their compensation—what they got out of it. There is no way that AVP could have spread around the planet the way it did if each new country that picked it up had to raise thousands of dollars to finance it.

Is there no paid employee?
Initially we had some staff in the yearly meeting office—Lee Stern

was extremely helpful. For a while, in 1984–86, I was paid to go into the yearly meeting office in New York City and handle administrative details for AVP. And in the '90s, we hired an executive director. But we've gone back to volunteer leadership. We found ourselves putting too much energy into raising the funds to pay for that position, which deflected us from just spreading the program.

As I said, going into the prisons was happenstance. I don't think we thought we were setting up a program that would spread throughout the prisons in the United States. We had a Quaker worship group in Greenhaven Prison that had, as part of their program—in addition to a half-hour worship—a half-hour discussion time. During the latter, one thing we'd do is tell the men what other things Quakers were doing that might be of interest to them. We told them about what Quakers had done during the Vietnam War, how we'd traveled all around the United States training individuals in ways to enter demonstrations and keep them nonviolent. Philadelphia was one of the areas. We did that work coast to coast. Trained thousands.

There was a group of men in the prisons called the "Think-Tank Concept." They were trying to work with. . . .

These were prisoners?
Yes. They were trying to work with youth from New York City who were on a violent track, to lead them to other ways of addressing their problems without violence. And they didn't feel they were having as much success as they would have liked because what they were predominately working with was fear. They'd bring these young fellas in and try to scare the daylights out of them—tell them how horrible prison was and if they continued what they were doing they were going to end up there. It wasn't working.

Was this before the first AVP workshop?
Oh yes.

And was this the group that then approached you?
Yes. When they heard about our involvement in the Vietnam War demonstrations they said, "Well is there something that you could teach us that we could then pass on to these younger guys?" We said we could

do a workshop for them. So the first workshop was born.

Did the think-tank then become part of AVP or did it retain a separate existence?

They continued separately, but it was largely members of that group who came into the first workshop: about eight men. And it also happened in Auburn Prison. There was a Quaker worship group and a similar process up there.

How would you describe the relationship between AVP and Quakers?

Well, I've always felt that I wanted AVP to become ecumenical, totally so, and not just be a Quaker program. I think that is true in many of the places where it's gone, and I know in New York state that the people we trained to be facilitators were of all denominations or none at all. And I'm assuming that's happening in other places as well because while Quakers can give the initial push, there's no reason they should claim it as just their territory.

Have inmates become trainers or involved in organizing AVP?

We believed that unless we could bring the participants to the trainer level of participation, this program couldn't have the kind of outreach that we were aiming for. So whenever we went into a prison for the first time, we tried to complete all three levels of the workshop: basic, second-level, and training for facilitators to get individuals who are trained as apprentice facilitators. And from then on, when we went into the prison we would have a mixed team of inside facilitators and outsiders. Early on we set the policy that we would not support workshops that only had inmate facilitators, not because we didn't trust their capacity to lead the workshop—in fact I think that some of our very best facilitators have been from the inside—but we soon realized there was pull from the administrative side in prisons to get involved and take this over as one of their programs. We never wanted AVP to be a program of the prison system. We wanted it to be a program coming in from the outside, from individuals who were there because they were concerned. We wanted it to be a program that belonged to the participants. When I go in and do a first workshop, I say to any group that I'm here as a volunteer because I want to give a gift to them that was given to me. And that really seems to have an impact. I can't consider that I'm giving them a gift if I'm paid. We do, however, try to cover expenses for facilitators: travel, babysitting costs, etc. This is a problem of some controversy because guys come out of prison and need money. So we make some exceptions based on need.

So AVP, you say, started by happenstance in prisons, but the workshops go far beyond that. How did that happen?

In order to do prison programs you have to do outside programs first. You have to train people on the outside because every workshop in prison needs an outside facilitator. So there's always been a strong citizen component, or outside people component to AVP, because that was necessary in order to do the programs in the prison. We've always done sample workshops, for instance, at FGC gatherings, as a step forward to enabling people to then take the program into the prisons, where it started.

Worldwide application began in the late 1980s. My wife died in 1988, and in 1989, Friends from abroad were writing and saying, "Why don't you come visit us?" And I thought, why not? And as this thought began to mature in my mind, I thought, why don't I share AVP while I'm there? Also, in 1989, Ellen Flanders and Janet Lugo went to England to share the program. Then, late in the 1990s, during the crisis in Yugoslavia, there was a lot of community violence, and I saw no reason why AVP shouldn't have applicability in that culture as well as in the prison culture. I learned that there was a Quaker in Yugoslavia who'd set up what he called the Baranja International Meetinghouse who was trying to work with Croatians in the Baranja region to help bring about more peaceful ways of solving their conflicts in the future.

A Yugoslav national?

No, a British Friend, Nicholas Street. I offered to go over and give a workshop. And I've been doing that ever since. And this fall it looks like we'll be going back to do some workshops in Serbia because we had some Serbian folks here and did a workshop with them, and they said, "Oh, we need this!" and "Won't you come to Serbia?" Now the work in the former Yugoslavia is taking a turn toward doing prison workshops—they have prisons there and feel the need for that work, too. But my purpose in going there was to help the people of the country to recognize that there were other ways of dealing with problems than resorting to violence and war.

Is there a partner organization there?

Yes, the Evangelical Theological Seminary in Osijek, in Croatia. And the person there, Michelle Kurtz, is a Presbyterian missionary from the Midwestern United States. She's been our primary contact, but now that I've been back there five times, planning a sixth, we have contacts that are strictly Croatian, Serbian, and so forth. It's viewed very much as a community program as well as one that could be suitable in their prisons. We did a workshop in a refugee camp in Gascini, in Croatia.

I know AVP has been active in Africa. Is it spreading around the world?

Oh yes, it's on six continents, all of them except Antarctica. In 1988, I attended the triennial sessions of Friends World Committee and there I offered a sample workshop on AVP. Val Ferguson asked if I'd be interested in representing Friends at the NGO Alliance on Crime Prevention and Criminal Justice at the United Nations in New York, an activity that the Quaker UN Office didn't feel it could take under its wing. So I became the Quaker representative to this alliance, which holds a worldwide Crime Congress every five years. This body planned and conducted ancillary meetings of the congresses on subjects pertaining to criminal justice. I offered to do one on AVP. The first Crime Congress I attended was in Havana, Cuba, and we held an ancillary meeting there on AVP and there seemed to be considerable interest. One man there was from Colombia and wanted to know if I could come there to share AVP and so forth. I developed world contacts through that venue. The next Crime Congress was held in Cairo. By then I'd been attending meetings for seven or eight years. It seemed to me that if we were going to tackle the problems of crime worldwide, we had to look beyond prisons because that's not the best way to tackle the problem.

After the fact, as opposed to being more proactive?

I wanted to see, on the worldwide level, a focus on alternatives. Now I see this happening in the Great Lakes project in Africa (Burundi, Uganda, Kenya, and Rwanda). In 1995 we introduced AVP into Africa, first in Kenya, then Uganda and South Africa. There have also been extensive trips to Central America, Europe, Australia, and New Zealand. British and Australian AVPers have taken it to India. I think AVP has appropriate application all over the planet.

What could we do that's more constructive than just sending people to prisons? At the Cairo congress, this all became very clear to me—that we were focusing too narrowly. I got back to New York thinking we need to do work on restorative justice: ways of dealing with individuals committing crimes before they get into prison and perhaps eliminating the necessity to put them in prison. This is a process whereby all the parties with a stake in a particular offense come together to resolve collectively how to deal with the aftermath of the offense and its implications for the future. When I brought this up at the NGO Alliance meetings in New York, they decided to set up a working party on restorative justice. And since I had opened my mouth, I became the chair. For the next five years, until the next congress in Vienna, we put in a good deal of work developing this whole topic for UN consideration. We generated a report, and the alliance accepted it and submitted it to the crime commission of the UN, which they accepted and put on the agenda of the UN general assembly. It was approved as a project for the section that works on these matters. So, the UN adopted restorative justice as something it would support and promote worldwide. At that point I decided I'd done my piece, so I resigned from the NGO Alliance, and Paul McCold from Lehigh Valley (Pa.) Meeting has taken on this work.

How does AVP keep track of all the activities? I noticed in the website description that AVP continues to increase at a rate of 30 percent a year, which is phenomenal, and I wonder how an organization doing that well keeps track of all its different parts—doesn't it need to?

We have a national gathering once a year and an international gathering every second year. AVP groups from other countries volunteer to take responsibility for the international gathering. In the United States, we need a board in order to qualify for nonprofit, tax-deductible status. So we have a designated president/clerk and a vice president/assistant clerk. They have virtually no duties until we hold the annual meeting, and then they clerk it. But we do have a committee that is representative of all the individual regional units throughout the country, and they, like other committees, mostly conduct their business by telephone conference and e-mail.

They are getting permission to be in prisons and communicating with them?

Yes, and with people around the state who were doing AVP and getting their reports. We had a report system that wasn't working too well. That's one place where the volunteer aspect failed.

The Internet has helped tremendously with the communication between the various units. It grows rapidly because as people experience it and want to see it carry on, there's no door or portal they have to go through; they can just say, "Send us stuff." We have a volunteer in Vermont who handles distribution of all of the printed materials that we have. So the newsletter, the *National Transformer*, is a major communication vehicle for people in the United States. All of the countries where it's taken root have developed their own distribution system for literature, but a lot of them turn to the United States for materials. Many countries have newsletters of their own.

As you look to the future of AVP, what are your greatest hopes and fears?

My greatest hope is that it can be accepted as broader than just prison work and be a significant factor in helping to bring about a more peaceful planet. I think it's applicable to human nature at all age levels. The Help Increase the Peace Program (HIPP), under American Friends Service Committee, is a version of AVP for teenagers. If you get their manual and look at it, you'll see it follows the AVP program very closely. I'd also hate to see it become commercialized. I can believe that there are situations where perhaps we should consider compensation of facilitators, but I think one of its great strengths has been that people do it because they believe in it and get something out of it themselves and they want to help others, not for any monetary compensation that they might get. In the prison setting, the prisoners have said that the fact that facilitators coming in are volunteers makes the program more believable and acceptable. Once you start paying people, it can still do good, but it would become like all the other programs out there where people are getting paid to facilitate. I would hope that AVP could maintain its strong level of volunteerism.

October 2002

Transformation of Violence

by Harold Wilson

Where does it come from—this powerful rush of emotion and adrenaline that society labels as violence? Nothing has ever been created that did not possess something of its creator. Is humankind the originator of violence or does it come from the creative force of the universe? Call that creative force and power anything you wish, some of it belongs to all of us. That power is able to change people or situations by either a caring attitude expressed through creative actions, or by massive destruction and cold-heartedness.

It feels like a million years ago when I was just a "fish"—prison slang for any new inmate, since most newly incarcerated people feel and act like a fish out of water and are too often easy prey for the "sharks" who are the predators of prison—and I came face to face with violence. It came at me for no discernible reason or cause, at least that a fish like me could see.

I had experienced violence in my life before coming to prison—violence of my own making and thinking. But seldom, if ever, had I been hit in the mouth for refusing to give some guy some of my canteen food, or for refusing to perform any one of a hundred sexual acts, or just for being "fresh meat." But prison changed all that and changed me, in some ways for the better but mostly for the worse.

The threat of violence in prison permeates every minute of your life. It is always there, lurking in the next bunk, or behind the corner of the chapel, or there in the shower with you. Even the accidental bumping of a bunk can get you hit upside the head with a steel chair in the hands of the man you are locked in with every single night.

These experiences, and a million more, some as apparently harmless as hearing the sound of a bullet whizzing by your head that was fired to break up a fight in the yard, change even the most gentle person. They destroy the trust you have in others, and that others have in you. The trust that the person you are sharing the shower with will not find you easy sexual prey. The trust that the guy who is being friendly to you and showing you around the prison yard won't try to steal your radio the minute your back is turned. Once trust is destroyed it is nearly impossible to rebuild or create it anew.

The repressive and confrontational atmosphere of prison creates and multiplies the stresses and tensions that promote violence. When a guard shakes down your cell and confiscates your TV because the cable connection has been repaired or looks altered somehow, your first thought is one of violence and vengeance. You feel that something that cost you nearly a year's wages, by prison standards, has been stolen from you for no good reason at all. Staff can lie and be abusive, uncaring, or downright lazy—anything to protect easy kickbacks and authoritarian image.

There are painfully few ways in which being incarcerated helps the rehabilitation process of a prisoner. There are a very few mental health treatment programs that help one or two prisoners change for the better and rethink the violence they have relied on for so long to survive and resolve conflicts in life. Some powerful tranquilizing drugs produce personality changes in some violent prisoners, but in most cases they either end up as zombies or wired monsters, ready to snap at any moment. Some of the best help toward rehabilitation comes from volunteers who come into prison as a part of self-improvement groups such as AA, religious fellowships, and other inmate cultural clubs and groups. These precious people have the one essential quality that 99 percent of all prison staff are lacking—they actually care about people who are locked up, both while they are still inside and also once they are returned to society.

Most prison staff seldom, if ever, care about a prisoner's rehabilitation. In fact, most staff do not use that word anymore, since most believe it's either impossible for a prisoner to be changed and be rehabilitated, or they simply don't care if that prisoner returns to society as a bitter, vengeance-seeking monster—one they helped to create through abuse, repression, racism, mental torture, or physical brutality.

We all have the power to transform or bring about change and self-rehabilitation. There are many tools that we can use. You would be surprised how far a caring attitude and concern for the welfare of others can go toward preventing violence—both violence within one's own life and the violence everyone comes face to face with every day.

One example of this transformative power involves a woman in New York City named Marge Swan. One dark night Marge was returning home across Central Park to her apartment, carrying a heavy load of books in both arms. She heard footsteps behind her and a big man came up and crowded her to one side. "Hold-up!" she thought. But in a flash of transforming inspiration, she turned to the man and said, "I'm so glad you came along, my arms are aching from carrying these books. Won't you carry them for me?" She dumped the whole load of them into his arms.

To her surprise, he took them. They walked together to the door of her apartment and she held out her arms for the return of her books, saying, "Thank you so much, you helped me so much." The man replied lamely, "Lady, that wasn't what I was going to do." By calling on the hidden "better side" of her potential assailant, Marge not only avoided being mugged, but enabled him to be a more considerate and caring person than even he thought he could be.

Gandhi, Martin Luther King Jr., and their followers demonstrated that it is possible to transform violence into peace and nonviolence by facing suffering and possible death to gain a principle, and to do so without returning violence for violence. In this way, they forced recognition of their causes and thus won allies and victories without violence.

A person is no less a person when walking away from a conflict or handling it with humor rather than by resorting to violence. One is no less a person when permitting an adversary the opportunity to save face in order to maintain dignity and retire from a stressful and potentially violent confrontation with a win-win solution.

Gandhi's and King's approach to potential violence requires thought before action and listening, not merely hearing. It requires that we be ourselves rather than an uncontrolled person under the influence of emotions, environment, alcohol, or drugs. It necessitates weighing the cost of our actions and being concerned for their consequences.

Today you read and hear about people who say that they would not feel it necessary to carry a weapon if it were not for the fact that the environment is full of armed people looking for a chance to kill or rob a defenseless person. "You have to fight fire with fire," you may hear them say. How mistaken they are! Everybody knows that you don't fight fire with fire; you fight fire with water! The water of nonviolence that quenches the fire of violence, defuses bombs, cools hot tempers, reduces tensions, and takes away all fear and hostility with an attitude of caring and good will.

There are causes for which one is willing to suffer and even die. This was the case with Gandhi's struggle for the independence of India, with King's demonstrations for civil rights in the South, and most recently with Mandela's fight for freedom in South Africa. But it is hardly considered right or appropriate to offer up your life trying to protect the contents of your pocketbook.

Every person needs to search deeply for the right tactics and follow the most inspired and intelligent leadership available. Before Gandhi started what perhaps was the most important and effective demonstration of his life—his famous march to the sea, which touched off the national protest against the salt laws of India—he spent two months in seclusion, searching inwardly for the most transforming tactic to fight this kind of repression. He found it! All people need to take the time for this kind of deep searching.

Participants in Dr. King's march on the capitol of Alabama were not regarded as weaklings or cowards because they suffered the attacks of mobs and police dogs without fighting back. They did not allow themselves to be discouraged or pushed back from their goal of marching to the city of Montgomery. Their courage and determination drew supporters from all over the country, and finally forced the authorities to summon the National Guard to protect them. This became the turning point of the Civil Rights Movement in the South.

The society we live in is responsible for the existence of crime and criminals because, to a point, criminal activity is a product of social disorganization. Our society is one of the most violent in the world. This tragic level of violence among our people is in part a response to the violence embedded in our institutions and in our values. Some people, more than others, are entrapped by this violence and find that it fills their lives with trouble. But there is no one among us that does not share the capacity for violence, and there is no one who is not hurt by it, one way or another.

I do not believe that people should live this way, nor do I believe that they must accept a society that is partially responsible for crime. Even if it is, I don't think that this lessens the individual's responsibility for one's own actions. But I do know that the transforming power that Gandhi and Dr. King used so effectively still has as much power for us in today's world. This power is well able to transform hostility and destructiveness into cooperation and community, while still doing true justice among us. I believe it is possible to tune in to this power, and that if we do, it will enable us and our opponents to realize our birthright of peace and dignity. I believe that there are certain individual and group dynamics that make it possible to effectively direct this power; and that these dynamics can be learned and used by all people everywhere to build more constructive lives and healthier societies.

In my own life I have discovered that one of the ways to use and direct this power is through the Alternatives to Violence Project (AVP). At first AVP's focus was on prisons and helping to reduce the level of violence in the prison environment, both to help prisoners survive prison and, at the same time, to deal with violence when they are confronted with it directly, in prison or back in society. The AVP guidelines that I have learned are:

Seek to resolve conflicts by reaching common ground.

Reach for that something in others that seeks to do good for the self and for others.

Listen. Everybody has made a journey. Try to understand where it is the other person is coming from before you make up your mind.

Base your position on truth. Since people tend to seek truth, no position based on falsehood can long prevail.

Be ready to revise your position if you discover it is not fair to all.

When you are clear about your position, expect to experience great inward power to act on it. A response that relies on this power will be courageous and without hostility.

Do not expect that this response will automatically ward off danger. If you cannot avoid risk, risk being creative rather than violent.

Surprise and humor can help transform violence into nonviolence.

Learn to trust your inner sense of when to act and when to withdraw.

Work towards new ways of overcoming injustice. Be willing to suffer suspicion, hostility, rejection, and even persecution if necessary.

Be patient and persistent in the continuing search for injustice.

Help build a community based on honesty, respect, and caring.

Build your own self-respect.

Respect and care about others.

Expect the best.

Ask yourself for a nonviolent way. There may already be one inside you.
Pause and give yourself time before acting or reacting. It may make you
open to nonviolent transformation.
Trust your inner sense of what's needed.
Don't rely on weapons, drugs, or alcohol. They weaken you.
When you have done wrong, admit it, make amends, and then let it go.
Don't threaten or put down.
Make friends who will support you. Support the best in them.
Risk changing yourself.

Transforming power feels like, "*Aha!!!*" because with it you can sense a
spirit of caring. There is a real letting go of something (feelings, patterns,
grudges, etc.). You will feel a sharing of something. You will feel right
about it. You will lose your fear if you had any to lose in the first place.

Conflict in social action comes in many forms: brute force, implacable
institutions, internal divisions among one's friends, just to name a few.
If there's an opening in the situation, a way through toward resolution,
we're going to have to be very quiet so as not to be at the reactive mercy
of each opposing thought. We have to listen very carefully for this unique-
ness of each individual, including ourselves and all the various levels of
our being. We also must listen for the way that fear and polarization
from outside reflect what is within us all, and for ways in which we can
do what we do with each other, but without putting the other person,
friend or foe, out of our hearts.

It takes the split-second timing of the quiet mind, like Gandhi's or
King's, working in harmony with an open heart, to know just when and
how to say, "Hey!" to a potentially dangerous opponent. So we work
to be clear enough to seize the time. If you're a union leader in a tough
collective bargaining session, for example, you'll want to catch that moment when it is best to yield a little, or when to shake your head saying,
"No deal!" If you're working in a nonviolent peace movement, timing
will be crucial in deciding when to call for national legislative opinion,
when to confront the central government, when to march to the next
Montgomery, and when to walk to the sea once more. With the future
of the human race at stake, we need to strengthen that precious awareness that allows us to take in all the elements of our world's situation.

Seeking Peace in Wartime

L ooking through old FRIENDS JOURNALS, readers can find many articles by conscientious objectors, all of them moving accounts of aspects of an objector's journey—family and economic difficulties, struggles with ostracism in home communities and in the communities where objectors were sent, experiences in mental institutions or on farms, dismay at personal conflicts of heart and mind, or the sufferings of one who has been forced into the army and still will not carry a gun even as his superiors constantly mistreat him. For this volume, we are printing three. As with other topics in this anthology, there were many excellent articles to chose from; however, for this volume we have chosen those that represent recent wars: one is an overview, with personal examples, of conscientious objectors in World War II; one about a young man whose father and brother had served in the military and who himself signed up during high school but finds that after enlistment he had never considered the actual fact of killing another human being; one written by a young woman who joined the army during the Gulf War as a combat medic. She finds that she had no idea that she would be drilled to see other people as objects and to experience the adrenaline rush and "blood lust" of killing indiscriminately. Nor did she realize that her job was not to save lives but to let the worst die while she patched up the least injured to rejoin the battle. Friends advising conscientious objectors today often find that they are working with young people such as the latter two.

The next article is a brief look at the idea of "just" war, a concept still embraced by the Catholic Church and a concept often thrown up as a foil to those who would argue against war. Following that, Newton Garver, in his essay "Some Thoughts on Peace and Justice," helps readers to look critically at the words "just" and "justice" to determine more clearly what we imply when we use them. Newton's admonishment to "plain speaking" and clear practice takes us to the heart of why the Peace Testimony must be grounded in spiritual seasoning.

Finally, a touching essay by a survivor of the Nagasaki atomic bomb blast offers insight into the meaning of peace in wartime.

S.H.

December 2006

U.S. Conscientious Objectors in World War II

by John Mascari

World War II was a very important period in the history of U.S. conscientious objectors. When the draft was activated, it was the first peacetime draft in U.S. history, beginning before U.S. entry into the war. For the first time in a U.S. war, COs were permitted to serve their country not by being drafted into the military, but by engaging in alternative service called Civilian Public Service, or CPS. Also during World War II, the definition of CO was expanded to include religious persons who were not members of the three Historic Peace Churches (Friends, Mennonites, and Brethren). The passion of the World War II COs to serve their country in nonviolent ways during wartime continues to have an impact today.

A conscientious objector was any person who refused to participate in war because of his conscience. In legal terms, a CO qualified under the IV-E (now I-O or I-A-O) section of the Selective Service, which exempted men from combat service.

There are three main types of conscientious objectors. Noncombatants are those who will serve in the military but will not serve in fighting positions. Conscientious objectors also include people who will not serve in the military at all but will accept required alternative service. Finally, "absolutists" are those COs (not recognized by law) who will not register for the draft, not serve in any position in the military, nor accept alternative service.

During the 1940s, many factors influenced a person's decision to become a conscientious objector. Some people found that they could no longer fight after experiencing combat firsthand. More commonly, families influenced many COs. Some COs in World War II, such as Steve Cary and Asa Watkins, both well-known Quakers, were directly influenced by their fathers in their decisions to become pacifists. Steve Cary's father refused to work in a company making weapons, and Asa

Watkins' father refused to own a gun although it was the norm in their Southern culture.

Another major influence on conscientious objectors was their churches. Members of the three Historic Peace Churches were often raised with an understanding and expectation of pacifism. Some members of religious groups, including the Amish, may have felt pressured to register as COs because their church would otherwise have "disfellowshiped" them.

For some African Americans, such as Bill Sutherland and Bayard Rustin, pacifism, combined with a strong sense of the injustice suffered by blacks in the United States, helped influence them to declare them-selves conscientious objectors in World War II. Bayard Rustin wrote a letter to his local draft board in 1943 explaining why he could not serve: "Segregation, separation, according to Jesus, is the basis of continuous violence…Racial discrimination in the armed forces is morally indefensible."

Throughout U.S. history, there have always been men who have refused to fight in wars because their consciences would not permit them to kill another person. Because religious principles figured strongly in the founding of the United States, there have always been people here whose religious beliefs prevented them from entering the military. Beginning with the Revolutionary War, military officers and the government have had to manage the issue of how to deal with those who would not fight.

During the Revolutionary War, Quakers were among the first conscientious objectors in the history of this country. COs did not support the war at all and indeed many remained politically neutral, siding with neither the British nor the Patriots. Quakers were absolutists who would not accept office on either side, refused to serve in the military, refused to pay someone else to take their place, and refused to pay a fine or a fee to the government. In addition, these war resisters refused to pay taxes to fund the war.

As the number of conscientious objectors increased during the Revolutionary War, the colonies imposed new penalties on them. A penalty of four months in prison was imposed on COs who refused to serve. Some COs were forced to serve in the army against their will. Some resisters were humiliated by being forced to march with rifles strapped to their backs. COs who refused to eat army rations went hungry. George

Washington personally released some of these COs when they were brought to him at his home.

There were also conscientious objectors during the Civil War. In the South, COs were suspected of opposing both the war and slavery, and were viewed by some as "double traitors." Many Quakers endured jail and threats of death for refusing to fight in the war. Only 20 COs asked for noncombatant positions in the army.

As an alternative to fighting, Quakers worked to change society. Quakers were concerned with helping people escape slavery. They helped found the Underground Railroad, provided food and shelter to needy African Americans, opened schools for children, and assisted adults in need.

The First World War offered better alternatives for conscientious objectors than the Civil War, but it still provided a challenge to them. Unlike during the Civil War, where most men accepted jail sentences instead of noncombatant service, 20,873 men were granted noncombatant classification by their draft boards. This was in addition to 4,000 conscientious objectors who were members of the Historic Peace Churches and therefore exempt from fighting for their country.

In the early postwar years of World War I, many pacifists worked in Europe with American Friends Service Committee, providing relief to German war victims. During the interwar period, there was a growing peace movement in the United States, in part influenced by the activities of Mohandas Gandhi. Meanwhile, many U.S. citizens believed that there could never be another terrible war. There was a strong isolationist movement in the belief that this would protect the United States from another devastating war.

By 1940, U.S. views about isolationism were beginning to change. The Selective Training and Service Act of 1940 (the Burke-Wadsworth Bill) created the first peacetime draft in U.S. history. Prior to the start of this peacetime draft, Quakers, Mennonites, and Brethren worked together to negotiate the provisions of the pending Selective Service law. They requested a national register of COs, a civilian agency to administer the program, an alternative service option under civilian control, a national board of appeal, and a complete exemption for absolutists. The final law didn't go that far, but it did expand the definition of a CO from members of the Historic Peace Churches to anyone who could not fight because of religious training and belief. It offered the option for COs to perform work "of national importance" under civilian direction, an appeal process available under the Justice Department, and the right for violators to be tried under civilian courts rather than military court martial.

Since there was no national register of conscientious objectors, the total number is unknown, but 37,000 were classified by Selective Service as COs; 43,000 served as non-combatants; within the larger group of COs, 12,000 men served in Civilian Public Service; and 6,000 went to jail.

As alternative service, COs worked in forestry, as human testers, as firefighters, in farm work, and as hospital attendants in psychiatric hospitals. No matter what the job was, COs were always under the control of someone else and had to work without pay. For many COs, their work was boring, depressing, and unrewarding in that the U.S. public did not appreciate their jobs.

Many COs were in forestry, mostly under the control of the U.S. Forestry Service. It was the COs' job to build dams, levees, and reservoirs; dig ditches, clear channels, and sod gullies. COs were also responsible for a large amount of trail-clearing in national parks.

Because a war was going on, farmers needed help to produce their products and asked Selective Service to allow COs to help them. While most COs worked on dairy farms, others planted crops, picked vegetables, husked corn, dug potatoes, and pruned fruit trees, all for no pay. Veterans' groups protested that farming was too easy an alternative to military service and, as a result, stricter rules were set. For example, COs could not work within 100 miles of a family member.

Steve Cary, a Quaker World War II CO, said, "There is no doubt in my mind . . . that the greatest contribution which we made in that era was in the whole field of mental health." Some COs thought that working on farms was not work "of national importance," so they requested work in mental hospitals. In many cases they replaced workers who had enlisted or left these jobs due to the bad working conditions and low salaries. COs learned that the conditions in mental hospitals were appalling, and they committed themselves to establishing new standards for patients in mental hospitals.

All together, 3,000 COs worked in psychiatric hospitals, as ward attendants, mechanics, kitchen helpers, technicians, clerks, and outdoor laborers. These jobs of COs were sometimes dangerous. Some patients took their anger out on the COs by attacking them with knives. Despite these threats, COs felt that it was their responsibility to improve conditions in hospitals and find nonviolent ways to deal with patients.

One of the most dangerous jobs for COs was that of a human tester. These COs (about 500 COs volunteered) perhaps wanted to show their courage by offering themselves for hazardous experiments. The volunteers tested new drugs, extreme temperatures, and the effects of diseases such as jaundice, malaria, and pneumonia.

One of the experiments was a test seeking the mental effects of extreme diet deprivation of food and water. Thirty-six COs were tested for a 24-week semi-starvation experiment. They were limited to a calorie intake that was less than half of the 3,300-calorie diet given to a regular soldier and were required to maintain their normal physical activity. Overall, the COs' weight dropped by 22 percent. The CO human testing was kept a secret and almost no photos were allowed of the experimentations. Robert Wixom, one of the CO human guinea pigs, said, "We were there to do our duty and serve in a constructive, nonviolent manner."

Another service option for conscientious objectors was that of being a smokejumper who fought forest fires by jumping from planes. Many COs wanted to smoke jump, perhaps to demonstrate their bravery in the service to their country. Of the many COs who volunteered, only 240 were accepted for this dangerous job. During the fire season, these smokejumpers moved out West to camps where they waited until a forest fire started.

Noncombatant military service was another option for conscientious objectors in World War II who did not choose or were denied the opportunity for alternative service. Noncombatants were soldiers, but were exempted from using weapons, enabling them to receive military pay and benefits. Most of the 43,000 noncombatants were initially denied CO status by their local draft boards and then accepted non-combat positions. Some felt that being a noncombatant was a justifiable compromise. Most noncombatants were willing to be trained to use guns, but they just didn't use them. "Noncombatancy was also undeniably the service of choice for those who wanted to promote American victory, believed in the justness of the Allied cause, but felt constrained to nonviolence themselves," wrote scholar Cynthia Eller.

The last alternative for conscientious objectors was to serve time in prison. The lawmakers who created the Selective Service Act hoped that its provisions would mean fewer COs in prison than during World War I, but instead the number actually increased. The COs who went to jail were either denied CO status, refused to serve in a CPS camp, or never registered (only 300 were in prison because they didn't register). Jehovah's Witnesses accounted for the largest percentage of imprisoned COs. They requested CO status not because of an opposition to violence, but because they believed that the government had no right to draft them; they were denied. The maximum sentence for a CO was ten years and a $10,000 fine. Once out of jail, COs were at risk of being drafted and imprisoned again.

Conscientious objectors were often persecuted for their efforts in World War II. John F. Kennedy acknowledged this when he said, "War will exist until that distant day when the conscientious objector enjoys the same reputation and prestige that the warrior does today." World War II COs endured verbal abuse and vandalism of their homes, were refused service in restaurants, had to witness being hung in effigy, dealt with efforts to prevent them from voting, and were socially ostracized.

Conscientious objectors and their families also suffered economically. When the men of the family were in CPS, they were not paid. Many COs went on strike, and some called the workcamps "American Slave Camps." Families relied on the women to provide financial support. Also, families had to pay for COs to go into the CPS (about $35 a month). Finally, there were fewer job opportunities for the family members of COs because most of them would not accept employment that included working in war industries, and some employers refused to hire family members of COs.

Many CO families were separated while family members served in the workcamps or on farms. Some families disagreed with COs and were ashamed of what their relatives believed. In some instances, parents and spouses even threatened to commit suicide. The worry over persecution, loss of pay, and separation took over the lives of many COs' families.

Conscientious objectors also experienced delayed release from the Selective Service. Because veterans' groups objected to COs being released before people in active military service, the point system designed for fairness in determining terms of service in the military was not applied to COs. It was not until March 1947 that the last 360 COs in CPS were released, six years after the first CPS camp opened.

The contributions of WWII COs have had a lasting impact. Their efforts made positive changes in healthcare, in psychiatric institutions and prisons, and in the U.S. infrastructure. COs became leaders in U.S. social movements. They also played a large role in public health. From the experiments in which they participated, improvements have been made in the treatment of malaria, influenza, pneumonia, and jaundice. The starvation experiments offered information about the food and water needs of soldiers and refugees.

Conscientious objectors working in mental hospitals created new standards for the treatment of patients with mental illness. By exposing conditions in U.S. psychiatric facilities, COs were able to inform the public, which generated a demand for humane treatment of the mentally ill. Their efforts resulted in the establishment of the National Mental Health Foundation, which still exists to advocate for the rights of the mentally ill.

According to Austin Reiger, a Mennonite conscientious objector who was imprisoned, "The U.S. prison system is more in need of rehabilitation than all mental hospitals." Conscientious objectors worked against solitary confinement in prisons. Their efforts also contributed to the desegregation of federal prisons.

The concrete improvements conscientious objectors made to the U.S. infrastructure included their work to build highways, dams, and levees to control rivers, and to construct bridges.

Many people throughout history have seen COs as a nuisance, but their impact has been great. This is especially true for COs in World War II. This group of men clearly established that nonviolent alternative service is a patriotic substitute for war. During World War II, the public recognized that moral objection to government policy was acceptable. World War II COs were tolerated as expressions of democracy. The beginnings of the Civil Rights Movement and the acceptance of Gandhi's nonviolence originated at least in part among World War II conscientious objectors in the United States. COs became leaders of modern-day

U.S. social movements. Steve Cary became clerk of American Friends Service Committee, president of Haverford College, and a leader of the peace movement. Bayard Rustin was an organizer of the March on Washington, was an advisor to Martin Luther King Jr., and is now an inspiration to African American gay men. Conscientious objectors in World War II who served their time in jail helped end segregation in U.S. prisons. Desegregation in the U.S. armed forces can also be credited in part to the efforts of World War II COs. These COs paved the way for the many draft resisters during the Vietnam War and for tax resisters of recent years. As Rosa Packard, a contemporary Quaker tax resister, says, "The example and influence of World War II conscientious objectors helped clear this path for me." The example of these men and their commitment to nonviolence will inspire me to become a proud, patriotic conscientious objector.

A Gulf War Resister's Stand

by Aimee Allison

I had no idea when I joined the military what kind of training I'd have to go through. I joined as a combat medic, and I was thinking in the back of my head, "Well, I'll be helping people. I'm a non-combatant, so I won't be hurting anyone, right?" But at 17 I knew nothing about war, the military, the world, or myself. I had a Rambo-esque vision of what war would be like, a video-game mentality. It wasn't realistic.

In military training, I was given a big dose of reality. The line between combatant and noncombatant is very thin, if not nonexistent. In the military, the support system, which is everybody but the people who actually operate the weapons, is almost the entire military. As a combat medic, it's my job to support and to replenish the front battle lines. That's my job. So I can't separate being a medic from operating heavy machinery, from shooting somebody, from burning a village, or anything else.

Bayonet training was one of the earlier things that deeply disturbed me and set me thinking about the military. There are 300 women in my company: we're all in battle dress fatigues, with our M16s and bayonets. We're all out in this field in Fort Jackson, South Carolina. The drill sergeant stands up on a platform with a megaphone, instructing us how to jab, how to thrust, how to use the bayonet in the correct position. This is me—I've never been in a fight in my life. I've always been taught to talk things out. He says, "What's the spirit of the bayonet?" We're are forced to yell, "To kill, to kill, to kill with no mercy." He yells, "What makes the grass grow?" "Blood, blood makes the grass grow." We're supposed to make these noises. I just remember saying it, but I couldn't believe that I was saying it, because in church I learned that what makes us humane is mercy. That was my first step in realizing I had to be true to my own beliefs and my own sense of right and wrong.

They tried very hard in the military to make every one of us lose our own identity, to make us afraid to question authority, to follow orders blindly, and to look at the enemy not as a human being but as an object. There are people who are deeply disturbed as individuals, and some take action and some of them don't. But on some level, most people in the military think about what they're doing and either choose to follow their conscience or not.

Other things that we did were equally disturbing—like shooting M60s, which are huge machine guns, at human-shaped targets. I have a friend who just came back from the Persian Gulf War and saw a lot of things. One of the things that he saw was Kuwaiti troops using M60s—they're supposed to be used on buildings or tanks—shooting Iraqi soldiers. All he saw was red mist—it decimates people. Right now, actually, he's receiving psychiatric treatment, because to see that destroys part of your own humanity. I know I did the right thing in refusing to be part of that. He also saw the French Foreign Legion massacring Iraqi troops—because they don't take prisoners. We won't read about these things in the paper for 20 years.

When my unit was activated, they took a piece of the unit—psychiatrists, psych doctors, psych nurses, and other people. They told them that there had been over 100 suicides of U.S. service people since the buildup. This was before the war started. I never read in the paper about any suicides of U.S. service people—I know that. People tried to deal with their conscience or the situation in different ways, and one of them was by committing suicide.

Another thing that happened in the development of my conscience was the positive reinforcement of learning about nonviolence, learning about Martin Luther King, Jr. and Gandhi, and the power of nonviolence to change situations. I still believe that nonviolence is the answer in the Israeli-Palestinian conflict too. I consider my being a CO as an extension of King's nonviolent movement.

The third thing that changed my way of thinking about the military was my training as a medic. As a military medic, my job is not to help people. The entire purpose of a medic is to continue the military mission. So if I see, after all the bombs are dropped in a battle, that there are several soldiers down, it's my job as a medic to assess every man or woman who's injured and establish priorities for evacuation based on the injuries, a procedure known as triage. Those people who are least injured I treat first, because they are most likely to return to their duty stations. The people who are most injured—if I don't have time after treating the least injured—I give a shot of morphine. Then I put them behind the screen and allow them to die. That is my duty as a medic. In the civilian world, if there's an earthquake or a fire, you treat the most injured first because they're most likely to die first. That's not the way it is in the military, because the truth is that the military not only doesn't care about the people it drops bombs on, but it doesn't care about its own side either. We're just cannon fodder; we're just part of the machine. I remember even the officers in my unit saying, "I know this is wrong, it seems wrong—but it's your job."

When a lot of people were leaving, I remember one physician, an OB-GYN woman, who said, "I don't support this war; it's a ridiculous war, a war for oil—why, what's the purpose?" But when her number was called, she went. I talked to her on the phone the night before she was to go. I said, "You know, you don't have to do this." She said, "Well, Aimee, I have my career riding on this."

Every person in the military, or in society in general, has faced at some point the question: am I going to do what I know is right? A lot of the COs I've met, even people who went to prison, say that if they had known about the opportunity for discharge, they would have done it a long time ago. Even though the U.S. military has these regulations through which to apply, it's very difficult to prove to the military that you're sincere and that you're a true CO. In many ways, the military disrespects the UN's recognition of CO so troops are still being sent to the Middle East. There were a few parades—Oh, everyone's home!—but there are still people over there.

There's sort of a move to the right, a wave of patriotism, all these yellow ribbons, the flag waving, the 50th anniversary of Pearl Harbor—all this stuff. It's all part of the same movement to the right, and it's a very scary feeling for me, because it means that mainstream America is not thinking and not questioning authority. That can only have bad repercussions for democracy, which thrives on different points of view. I think that in a time of great patriotism, in this wave of Follow the Leader, people should help to try to right the wrongs in the country and in the world.

From my perspective, if I were 17 and had to do the whole thing again, I would have appreciated it if just one person would have said,

"You know, you want to go to college, you want to be in politics, you want to do all these great things, Aimee, but why would you dedicate eight years of your life to an institution whose sole purpose is to kill people?" If they would have asked me that, maybe I would have thought twice about joining. That's what I want to do: at least put my viewpoint out there, even though it doesn't come near to equaling the millions of dollars of advertising from the military.

December 15, 1977

A Moral Objection is Enough

by Robert Seeley

He is young, and a bit frightened, and trying hard not to show it. It is as if he cannot get comfortable, cannot bear to look at me, cannot stop his hands from picking up first a sheet of paper, then the ashtray next to him on my desk, then a book.

I ask his name, his address, and where he is stationed, noting his responses as fast as I can. Then I suggest, as I usually do, that he tell me what his problem is.

The words come out in a rush, in that strange mixture of military alphabet soup and street language common to many enlisted people. GITMO, Med Cruise, MARGE, TDY, XO—I can't follow it all; he is speaking so fast and with such assurance in a speech totally foreign to my civilian mind. I have to stop to translate even now, when I have heard this language a hundred times or more.

But his problem is clear: it is the Navy. He has been in a little over a year, and three months ago he decided he couldn't take it any more. So he left. He is back now—he turned himself in two weeks ago—and facing court-martial. He doesn't know when, or what level, or how much he might be punished. At the moment he is waiting.

He has been here before, but it was after office hours, and the one person in the office could only talk with him briefly and give him some literature. The literature makes things easier: he knows how he might get a discharge, and we can quickly eliminate the ones that don't apply.

I ask about his family, his medical problems, his military record, and whether he has any psychological problems. Nothing worth pursuing.

His enlistment was the usual story: he signed up on Delayed Enlistment while he was in high school, took a summer to go to California, and came when the Navy called. The recruiter promised him trips around the world, good pay, an exciting life, and training in nuclear power if he qualified. He didn't qualify. Now he is a cook.

Did he have a criminal record, I ask? Nothing. He grew up in a rough neighborhood, but he usually kept out of trouble. Once he was in a car where the police found some hashish, but the charges were dropped.

Did he use drugs? Not to speak of—once in awhile he experimented, nothing stronger than hashish. But he didn't tell the recruiter about it.

I am searching, almost desperately, for a way to keep him out of court.

Did he get any promises in writing from the recruiter? Only the usual ones on the enlistment contract.

It is no good. His enlistment was probably legal. His best court defense is unlawful enlistment; without it or another defense, his chances of conviction are over 90 percent. I drop it for the moment. Perhaps his records will show something he doesn't remember.

How does he feel about conscientious objection, I ask, feeling a bit awkward? It is always like this, no matter how many times I ask it. Conscientious objection is not just another grounds for discharge. It is a philosophy of life, a way of life, and the question I am asking is really about who he is and what he cherishes most. I cannot ask it lightly, and I always flounder a bit.

So does he. He wants to be a conscientious objector, he says, but he isn't sure he qualifies. Where before he had spoken quickly, angrily, and assuredly, he has become quiet and hesitant.

Why not, I ask?

He is not religious, and the regulation requires religious training and belief. He thinks he may not object to all wars, and the regulation requires him to. No one he knows would give him a supporting letter.

He is going on to list more problems with his beliefs. I have been writing furiously, trying to keep up with the flow of his words, but now I abandon my notebook. One can't write and talk—or listen.

I reflect again, as I often have before, what an awesome business conscientious objection is. It would be easy for a clever person to construct a fraudulent claim, but few do. I can recall one that I was sure of, two or three that I suspected. For the rest, they were sincere, and, oddly, would not submit a claim if they were unsure of their own motivation. It makes counseling, often, a very long process, for no one is as sure as some objectors would like to be. But there is something forbidding, almost sacred, about conscientious objection, even to those who have just learned about it.

I wrench myself back to the conversation. What does he mean when he says he is not religious, I ask? What does he believe?

His story is one I have heard perhaps 40, perhaps 50 times, with variations. He was raised in a major church but has grown away from it. He does not criticize the church, though others I have talked with do; it simply began to mean less and less to him as he changed. Now it means little or nothing.

He is still telling me what he does not believe. That is the easy part—it is much harder to state a positive belief—but it is also necessary. He is clearing away underbrush to plant an oak.

He falters and stops, looking at me now as though I can tell him what he needs to say. I am recalling my own struggle to state my beliefs without trivializing them. Telling him what to say would mean telling him what he believes, who he is. His claim, if he makes it, must be his. It would be easier in many ways if he could simply invoke a creed, but he is one who must find his own way.

His religion, I suggest, is whatever set of beliefs—whatever values, whatever God or non-God—rules his life most deeply. It has nothing to do with church-going or formal piety. There are church members whose religion is wholly different from their creeds, and there are non-church goers who are deeply religious.

The law can see, is allowed to see, no difference. Any strong belief, moral, philosophical, theological, is a religious belief for purposes of the law. The real question is why he feels as he does about war.

He is still bothered by the word. Forget about religion for a moment, I suggest. The law still uses the word, but the courts no longer require it. A moral objection is enough.

A moral objection is what he has. He is speaking more confidently now, of his revulsion to killing, of how when he was younger he went hunting and came back sickened. It is not, for him, a question of philosophy. He has no sophisticated rationale, no Scripture quotations, no church doctrine. He simply cannot, literally cannot, kill.

That is enough, I tell him, if it leads him to oppose war. But what did he mean when he said he did not object to all wars? When would he fight?

Suddenly I am struck by his youth. He is 18, perhaps 19 at the outside; an absurd age to carry his burden. He should be living, perhaps reading and studying war and peace at leisure, not struggling with such questions in a life-or-death situation. Philosophers do not resolve them in a lifetime; theologians have argued about them for centuries. Yet, as always, old politicians make wars, young soldiers fight them, and those young who question—who choose life instead of death, who refuse to die or to kill for distant reasons of state—those are the abnormal ones. They are the ones who must prove their case, as if war were self-evidently good and peace evil.

He is going on. He thinks he might fight if the country were attacked, but he is not really sure what he would do. He is perplexed by the war against Hitler. I have heard this, too, before. I have been through it myself. There are no answers, for one cannot be responsible for history or predict the future. There are only gropings toward answers.

Leaving aside the past and future, I ask, how does he feel now? He knows he could not kill, he says; he does not know how he would be in some other situation.

Then he should apply for discharge, I suggest, unless he feels dishonest in doing so. The law does not say he must think out all contingencies, or that he has to be a historian who has analyzed every situation. If he has, well and good; if he has not, neither have many others. He is in the Navy now, and he must hew to his own truth now, even if he does not understand that truth completely himself. That is bad philosophy, I reflect, but philosophers have time. They can argue endlessly over a point of ethics because they need not decide. They can wait for consistency because they will not die in battle, or kill, or go insane, if they do not achieve it in time.

He asks me, with an almost resigned air, about supporting letters. He will have problems, he repeats, getting any. He knows no one who could provide them. Maybe some friends in his old unit, a priest he knows. His parents? Not likely. His father was in the Navy; his brother did two years in Vietnam with the Marines.

We discuss it. After thinking awhile, he decides he can get four, perhaps five, letters. I am thinking how difficult all this must be for him. It is simple for one raised in an anti-war atmosphere to form an objection to war. The concept is not foreign; it does not mean violating all one's norms. For most people I have seen, however, it is no easy matter to oppose war. At best it means possible conflict with the family. At worst it can mean terrible self-doubt; am I really a conscientious objector, or am I just afraid of dying? All one's heroes may be military heroes. What other kind of courage does our society reward as highly?

He says nothing about this fear, so I say nothing. But I do not doubt that he feels it. He will not say anything, not yet, because admitting fear is not part of his code. One day, perhaps, we will discuss fear, and I may tell him he is displaying more courage than his brother who joined the Marines because his background told him to—or than I when I became a conscientious objector because it was natural to me. Perhaps I will be able to tell him that not to fear dying is a form of madness, a madness highly regarded in a culture which can kill hundreds of thousands at the touch of a button. Few are unafraid, for it is natural to be afraid. Often, those who are not, win medals and lose themselves when the shooting is over.

We discuss the questions he must answer in his discharge application. He has read them and found them confusing. I suggest that the problem is not in him, but in the questions. It is easy enough to state the nature of one's belief and to show how that leads to objection to war. That may entail struggle, but at least about how his beliefs have changed his life, about outward signs that he is an objector. This is impossible: there are no outward signs, and some actions he might take—such as disobeying orders—could lead to court-martial. He violates his conscience every day he remains in the Navy, yet he must remain in the Navy in order to get out.

Or here is a question on the use of force, with force left undefined. How is he to answer it and not appear a fool? I have seen people go round and round on this question, circling endlessly and getting nowhere because one can devise contingencies by the hundreds, plan responses to them, and find that the whole house of cards collapses in the event.

The crucial point, we agree, is that military force is different. It is planned, emotionless, calculated. One usually does not hate the enemy; one kills because that is the order. Hatred, patriotism, even the will to survive, may be there, but they are only instruments of a strategy. Military people are not violent, any more than the rest of us; they have families, most are kind to animals, few actually glory in the killing that is their trade. Yet they plan for, and are instruments of, the most horrific violence we know: indiscriminate, deadly, built on an honor and camaraderie that exclude compassion even for a respected opponent and expect none in return. Enforced with nuclear weapons, it is a code that can mean the end of us. Events have caught up with it, passed it and made it lethal, yet it still remains.

We have wandered off the track, but we are both learning. He is more relaxed than before, and I can talk about war and peace for hours with anyone who wants to talk.

What did I do? he asks. Was I in the military? I explain that I was a conscientious objector under the draft, that my local board recognized me, and that I did alternative service for two years. I add, only half-joking, that I sometimes wish they had turned me down at least once so I could have made an appeal.

It is half-past three, and he must get back to base for a muster. At the door he asks how long all this will take. I estimate three or four months, but it all depends how long he takes on his claim, how quickly he gets the required interviews, how overworked the Navy CO Review Board is this month or next. I suggest he try writing out answers to the questions and bring them back when he has them ready. Meantime I will find a lawyer to represent him. We shake hands, and he is gone.

April 1995

Comments on the Just War Theory

by Lincoln E. Moses

J ust war theory began with Augustine, got a boost from Thomas Aquinas, and has evolved over the centuries until the present day. A modern statement appears, including historical comment, in the pastoral letter of the National Conference of Bishops, May 3, 1983, entitled "The Challenge of Peace: God's Promise and our Response." As a form of moral discourse concerning war, the theory can attract sympathetic attention from people outside the Roman Catholic Church, including Friends.

I offer here my personal doubts about the usefulness of the theory, either in considering an impending war or judging a past one.

Somewhat varying statements of the just war theory can be found in various publications. I use the statement in the bishops' letter. It is recent, and it is a collective judgment. I take it to be a competent and authoritative statement. First, at paragraph 75, we find, "The council and the popes have stated clearly that governments threatened by armed, unjust aggression must defend their people. This includes defense by armed force if necessary as a last resort."

So, armed defense against "unjust aggression" is legitimate. Then, at 79, the transition to a statement of the just war criteria appears:

> In light of the framework of Catholic teaching on the nature of peace, the avoidance of war, and the state's right of legitimate defense, we can now spell out certain moral principles within the Catholic tradition which provide guidance for public policy and individual choice.

So the purpose of the theory is to "provide guidance," to policy makers and to individuals.

Section 3 comprises paragraphs numbered 80–110 and is entitled "The Just War Criteria." After historical background we come to:

> 84. the determination of when conditions exist which allow the resort to force, in spite of the strong presumption against it, is made in light of

jus ad bellum criteria. The determination of how even a justified resort to force must be conducted is made in life of the *jus in bello* criteria.

The latter encompasses two theses: first, that military means should be *proportional* to military objectives (don't use an atom bomb to blow up a bridge), and second, *discrimination* between military and civilian personnel should be observed. My quarrel relates not to these, but to the jus ad bellum phase, to which we now turn.

Under section 85 ("Why and when recourse to war is permissible"): The succeeding 14 paragraphs present seven criteria, which I list below, abridging but not changing the language.

86. a) Just Cause: War is permissible only to confront "a real and certain danger . . . ."

87. b) Competent Authority: War must be declared by those with responsibility for public order, not by private groups or individuals.

92. c) Comparative Justice: The question in its most basic form is this: Do the rights and values involved justify killing?

95. d) Right Intention: Right intention is relation to just cause; war can be legitimately intended only for the reasons set forth above as a just cause.

96. e) Last Resort: For resort to war to be justified, all peaceful alternatives must have been exhausted.

98. f) Probability of success: The purpose is to prevent irrational resort to force or hopeless resistance when the outcome of either will clearly be disproportionate or futile.

99. g) Proportionality: ". . . means that the damage to be inflicted and costs incurred by war must be proportionate to the good expected by taking up arms."

At first glance almost any of the above seems to be an appealing principle. But upon further examination they become more and more problematic. Let's consider them in turn.

Just Cause

To know whether there is a "real and certain danger" requires correctly understanding the opponent's capabilities and *intentions*. Further, a forecast of how things will unfold if arms are not taken up is needed. So this criterion is far from straightforward.

Competent Authority

This may be the issue at the core of the dispute, as with a revolution, or where a bi-fraudulent election clouds authority and at the same time threatens armed action. In our own country, there have been disputes between Congress and the President concerning authority to mount (or continue) armed action. In such straits, where lies competent authority? And upon whose say-so?

Comparative Justice

Clearly we have a matter of opinion (and religious conviction). What could be a true answer? How could it be found? Resolving this question satisfactorily seems as deep and difficult as deciding the main question: "Is war justified in this instance?"

Right Intention

Too often this must have a preordained answer (likely the same on both sides). How likely are we to find a policy-maker urging war *except* for "just cause"?

Last Resort

Once again, the opponent's capabilities and intentions are central. Once again implicit forecasts are of the essence. Additionally, "last resort" is likely to conceal tacit reservations about nonnegotiable items, such as talking with the opponent, or releasing hostages, or paying ransom for hostages, or. . . . In such straits the concept of armed force as a "last resort" becomes vague. A final complexity of this criterion is that it might justify preemptive action, thus clouding which party is defending.

Probability of Success

A frank forecast—and difficult one, for few human enterprises are more beset by randomness, surprise, and disappointment than is warfare. The criterion would offer more guidance if it spoke of a threshold for this probability. Is probability of 1/2 good? or bad? How about 3/4? or 1/4?

Proportionality

Here is a very hard question—perhaps as difficult as the main question. Whose lives count, and how much? How does loss (or gain) of territory count? What about national identity? And of course, both costs and gains need to be forecast before they can be compared.

I would summarize the objections above by saying that the theory necessarily depends on forecasts and other sorts of weak evidence, and so can offer little useful guidance, even in principle.

My next objections relate to the great operational difficulties just war theory must face due to practical factors, which are not treated in the theory. We live in an era when it is not far off the mark to say "information is power." On matters of war and peace, information is commonly corrupted by censorship, media control, self-serving news items, outright official falsehood, etc. So how is the conscientious citizen to apply these criteria with confidence in the result? The policy maker may have quite parallel difficulties, with deception of legislature and heads of state being all too common.

Just war theory has a long history; it was apparently designed to restrain monarchs' decision to engage in war. But even as Augustine's and Thomas Aquinas's justifications of slavery have become discredited, so, in my opinion, has just war theory become irrelevant (or misleading) in our age—if ever it was otherwise. The intrinsic obscurity of the theory and the treacherous fact base it must use make inferences based on just war theory fragile. Worse, it may bring net harm, partly by occupying time and effort that would better be spent in other ways to avert war; partly by its very name, which is easily and unconsciously received as an assertion that some wars, in this era of vicious, prolific killing, can be "just." Finally, if taken seriously, its effect is likely to strengthen the cause of war by raising morale of troops and citizenry—easily enough on both sides.

There is an additional cost to promoting the idea that some wars may be "just"; it supports reliance on war as a contingent instrument in international dealings—and corrupts those dealings. That reliance takes the edge off creative efforts to work through difficult tangles.

So, as the reader may surmise, I commend a hard look at just war theory before Quakers invest a scintilla of energy—or hope—in it.

Some Thoughts on Peace and Justice

by Newton Garver

The theme of the 1985 American Friends Service Committee Annual Public Gathering was drawn from Lucretia Mott: "There can be no true peace which is not founded on justice and right." It is a resounding slogan, and in one form or another, it has undoubtedly been part of the message of active Friends to quiet ones—both before and after the time of Lucretia Mott. It is a slogan which reaches out to oppressed peoples everywhere, helping to build a bond between us and them. And—partly for that reason—it reiterates a theme which has become increasingly strident in recent years, not only at Friends Center in Philadelphia, but among active and concerned Friends everywhere. I am concerned that this slogan is in danger of becoming creedal, that spotlighting the element of truth in this thought may have blinded some Friends to its limitations, and that the longing for settled doctrine, which lives in every human breast and which is perhaps sharpened in some by the absence of a Quaker theology, may be being filled by the dogma that securing justice is a prerequisite for securing peace in the trouble spots of the world, or by the false gospel that *everything* is after all really politics.

Lucretia Mott's remark is metaphorical and imprecise, but can be granted part of the truth. She speaks of "true peace," which may not be the same as actual peace in the real world. I suppose that true peace involves a robust and stable harmony of the legitimate interests of everyone. Since the only case where justice is lacking is when someone's legitimate interests have been thrust aside, it follows immediately that injustice is incompatible with true peace. This is something we must always keep in mind, and Lucretia Mott's remark is a fitting enough slogan for that purpose. That's the first principle.

There is also a second principal: demands for justice are not demands for peace. Nor is justice ever a *sufficient* condition of peace. For there can be no peace without compassion, without love, and without mercy. So we must be careful that the concern for justice does not blot out the need for compassion—and sometimes we may even need to let compassion and mercy blot out the demands for justice, as for example in the Middle East. This is equally true, and equally important. We must be careful not to let the one truth obscure the other.

Just as we cannot abide blatant injustice, so also we cannot allow the creation of a perfectly just society to become a precondition for peace. One reason is that there is constant disagreement not only about what is just in concrete cases but also about the very principles of justice. Even where the principles are not in dispute, as in the case of selling a secondhand car, we are daily witness to bitter disputes about just what rights the various parties have; that is to say, about what would be a just outcome. When it comes to principles, the disputes can be even more bitter, as when someone challenges whether ownership and occupancy over decades gives one a just right to land, or whether progressive (or nonprogressive) tax rates are just (or unjust). We must remember that there is a great difference in practice between justice and injustice: it is easy enough to agree in practice on many cases of blatant injustice, even when there is no consensus on the principles of justice—or even on what would constitute a fair resolution of the injustice. Where justice is abstract, injustice is concrete; that is why these two principles are both true. We must not let the application of Lucretia Mott's remark to the concrete cases of injustice beguile us into dogmatic abstractions which can only hinder efforts toward peace.

Another concern about declaring justice a precondition for peace is that we are apt to encourage those who will pursue justice with a sword. We should keep in mind that the rhetoric of justice is very powerful and is associated with urgency and necessity. Justice *must* be done, and be observed in the course of doing anything else. Our just rights cannot be left to the same sort of trade-offs and compromises as our dams and waterways. Nor can the rights of others. So when faced with denials and delays, the agents of justice among us have commonly resorted to coercion and the force of arms. If we say that justice must come *first*, do we not encourage such use of force? Can we expect either our allies or their opponents to interpret our rhetoric in any other way? I know that the Friends who insist on the priority of justice do not intend to give this sort of comfort to violence, but our actions are often other than we intend. The rhetoric of justice is so powerful, and historically has been so inflammatory, that we need to consider carefully its use, even when what we say is true.

In this connection it is worth noting that the words of Lucretia Mott conform as well to those protecting the status quo as to those seeking a new and peaceful socioeconomic order. President Reagan, for example, echoed them when he said, "True peace rests on the pillars of individual freedom, human rights, national self determination, and respect for the rule of law" (*New York Times*, November 15, 1985). I suspect that many Friends would agree that the words here serve to promote not peace but rather a standing justification (or rationalization) for not entering into a more peaceful relationship with the USSR, for not cutting the Defense budget, and so on. Reagan, for his purposes, could have expressed whole-hearted agreement with the theme of this year's annual public gathering! I believe that we should ask ourselves whether it is in conformity with the testimony of plain speaking to proclaim slogans which admit of serving such diverse interests.

A further consideration is that AFSC practice conforms to the second principle as much as Lucretia Mott's principle. Although we cannot be silent about injustice in South Africa or Chile, it does not help to stress justice in the work of the International Affairs representatives, or in the Middle East. If we were to say that justice is a precondition for peace in the Middle East, for example, we would only be fanning the flames of militants who are already overzealous. The most recent AFSC book on the Middle East does not call for a just peace but for *A Compassionate Peace*. And the reason is clear. The claims to justice—those put forward by the principal parties to the dispute about Jerusalem, the West Bank, and the Gaza Strip—are equally plausible and wholly incompatible. So peace requires that some of the claims to justice be given up and that some of the cries for justice be silenced.

How is that to be achieved? Not by censorship or tyranny, of course. One road would be to try to say what is really just, and then to argue the various parties out of some of their claims, to alter their picture of justice. That, however, is not a road any of us would much like to travel. It is so difficult to distinguish between a person's self-image and a person's sense of just rights, that our sense of solidarity with others normally leads us to suggest that they not insist on rights rather than they change their conception of their rights. So far the more promising road is to focus instead, as does the AFSC study of the Middle East, on the possibilities of compassion and cooperation. Most human beings are far more ready to admit that the others, too, are human and have human needs and aspirations than to admit that their cause has not been just. This is surely the case among Palestinians and Zionists. In such cases, peace depends on the prospects for compassion and cooperation—and in part on the prospects of compassion and cooperation suppressing the unanswerable questions of justice. In such cases the words of Lucretia Mott do not even seem true, let alone a self-evident dogma.

My concern is not to suppress the voice of Lucretia Mott—heaven forbid!—but to assure that her words are neither interpreted to condone or give comfort to the armed militants who echo them, nor interpreted to obscure the importance of compassion and cooperation as conditions of peace.

A third principle to bear in mind is that the practice of justice and the implementation of right depend on peace. They somehow depend, first, on the absence of war. The exact relation is difficult to state: justice and right tend to wilt during war and flourish only in its absence. The horrible camps and gas chambers of the Nazis could not have been set up and maintained if Germany had not been at war. The Japanese internment camps in the United States were similarly facilitated by war. Peace is not a sufficient condition of justice and right, but it seems a necessary one. It therefore remains true that one of the best ways to promote justice and right is to work for peace, e.g., by watering the feeble roots of compassion and cooperation.

I think the reason for the dependence of justice on peace is that justice and right depend in practice on there being sentiments of solidarity rather than enmity, or respect rather than hate. The very notion of "enemies" or people who are "evil" suppresses compassion and engenders horrendous sanctions for violence and injustice. It is only where there is a willingness to live together that people respect the rules for living daily. It is useful to conceive of peace (in a weak sense) as just the willingness to live together, whether because of our common humanity or because we are all children of God; and to conceive of true justice as principles of fairness which work in practice. Then we can see that the motto from Lucretia Mott is equally true if it is turned inside out: *There can be no true justice which is not founded on peace.*

Looking for Meaning

by Susumu Ishitani

I was in the eighth grade, at the age of 13, when I was exposed to the A-bomb in Nagasaki. I was talking with my elder sister in the dining kitchen of our house after coming back from school. We began to feel hungry and my sister had started cooking when we heard the buzzing sound of a U.S. bomber. My sister, who had experienced some terrifying air-raids before she came to Nagasaki city, immediately recognized the sound as that of the B-29 and suggested that we go to the shelter for safety. But I, who had not had any terrifying experiences of bombing, said, "Well, Sister, they just came again. They wouldn't do any harm. So far Nagasaki has never been badly attacked. So we shall be all right." Before I finished the last sentence, a strong glittering light struck us. I thought it was the light of a flash-light bomb dropped by mistake on the top of the roof of my house. I dashed into the next room, shouting out to my sister to come along, to hide myself from the light, proceeding to the corridor to get out of the front door. But before I reached the door, I felt a strong blast approaching, and I flattened myself on the floor. Soon I felt the blast arrive, smashing and blowing things around. I could not do anything but rely on God. In the moment when I felt the danger of death, a strong sensation of trusting God ran all through my body. It was a warm sensation like electricity, which made me feel that I would be definitely protected by God. Somehow I did not feel any fear. I concentrated all senses of awareness on the trust-feeling. Things were coming down near me. But I felt a kind of religious feeling and knew that I would not die, being protected by the divine power. . . .

As for my health, about half a year later I got blisters all over my body. The shape of those blisters was strange, looking like small round pancakes full of pus. I had swollen glands and a slight fever. Because of the dullness and fever from the blisters, I found it necessary sometimes to lie down on the floor without participating in gym class. When we were kept standing for a long time in line at school I sometimes felt dizzy and had to leave the line. This was for the few years when I was still in

Nagasaki. In those days I was apparently affected by the bomb, but we did not know anything of the effects of the radioactivity.

We sometimes hear people involved in peace movements in Japan say a phrase, "Hiroshima of anger and Nagasaki of prayer." Often when they say this, they mean that in Hiroshima, active peace movements come out of the anger of the victims of the A-bomb and in Nagasaki, people never stand up against anything but pray for help without doing anything positive, depending on either their fate or some authority. We cannot deny that in Hiroshima, we always find some activities regarding peace going on, while visitors to the A-bomb museum in Nagasaki find very few peace activities. But I wonder if anger can really produce anything of peace? How about prayer? According to my understanding, anger needs to be checked carefully so that it does not produce hatred, which is one of the elements of war. I can admit that indignation against injustice is necessary to create peace, which should be based on justice. The energy that comes out of indignation can be the source for the energy to push us to work for peacemaking. The energy to create anything has to be directed through the right channels. It cannot be creative if the anger is aimed at either American people or Russian people. Indignation has to be addressed to what cruel deeds we Japanese did just as equally to what the American military did, but not to military men as persons.

Human beings originally do not exist in solitude, separate from one another, but exist as social beings with warm feelings of humanity. The proof can be found among the suffering people in the situations under the mushroom clouds. When a father finally succeeded in getting out of the pile of fallen timbers and concrete things and found his wife unable to get out to safety from the approaching fire, he said, "I would stay with you and die together," after trying in vain to get her out. She said, "Save yourself, please, lest our children should be left without both parents." A boy who witnessed all of the tense situation of his parents' departure from one another has written describing what he has seen and heard. He was a sixth grader then. His father cried out and wept aloud while moving away from his wife and taking his son's hand. This boy lived to tell people about the A-bomb and not only about the ugliness of wars but about the beauty of human nature, too.

Out of such miserable situations some people have decided to make a new start in their life. They even say that it has to be made as a start of a new world for humanity.

For me, my A-bomb experience seems to be something given to me from which I am expected to draw meaning and power to live in such a way as to be an instrument of God or to show the glory of God. I do not think I have found all of the meaning or power that is expected for me to draw out of my experience yet. It must be an endless or bottomless source to draw out living water for me to look back or return in order to refresh my awareness that I live in the hand of God while being on the edge of the division of life and death. For we all live in such an existential condition in the nuclear age today. As we look at our living situation, we realize the development of science and technology has put us in a dangerous situation, as at any moment we might be killed by the explosive power of science and technology. Economic competition has put us in such a situation as we might be treating other human beings as tools and slaves without being able to treat others as persons who are as important and precious as we ourselves are. And the end of these trends leads us to wars and annihilation of humankind. We should have fully realized that we are forced by these conditions to be aware of the necessity of determining our decisive attitude to choose life rather than destruction even at the sacrifice of our easy ways of getting more material abundance, more convenience, and the superficial pride of being better than others in worldly life.

I happened to find myself in the historical event of the explosion of the A-bomb. A Japanese philosopher whom I know well is advocating his idea that the calendar year should start from 1945, when the nuclear age started, because it is so significant for human conditions in the history of humankind. I agree with him in the sense that the epoch-making event of the birth of possible self-annihilation of humanity urges us human beings to make radical changes for our survival, for finding a peaceful solution of conflicts, and for creating a new loving way shown by God in the way of Jesus Christ on the cross and on His resurrection. Light is going to be revealed by the darkness of the annihilating bombs to shine and show a new, caring way. We are in the middle of the time of awakening our souls to repent and change.

The other day, I found a poem in a Japanese Christian newspaper that expresses an important aspect of our search for meaning in our life. It goes like this, according to my English translation:

If not having become ill,
>   such prayers would not have come out.
If not having become ill,
>   such miracle would not have been believed in.
If not having become ill,
>   such divine world would not have been heard of.
If not having become ill,
>   such holy sacred place would not have been visited.
If not having become ill,
>   such a face would not have been gazed at.
Oh! Unless having become ill,
>   I would not have been able to become a human.

In our lives we have sorrows to face, and they come without our comprehension why they should come in our particular place, particular time, and to a particular person like you or me.

Sorrow, however, is good medicine for the soul. Those who do not drink from the cup of sorrow will never understand the significance of our life. Because of being in adverse situations, one can come to understand the importance of kindness to others. Having adverse, unfavorable experiences, one can come to know the truth which one will never be able to know through academic study or by common sense. One gains the power of courage to overcome the adverse situation and deepens the understanding of others who are in adverse situations.

Seeking Peace Through an Artistic Lens

Several profound poems, as well as "Dream: Antameruasiafricand," the latter written by a teenager, and the memoir of one who walked siently through "The Gates" in Central Park in February 2005, speak for themselves. We organize programs, analyze issues, write tracts and letters, build houses and inexpensive water filters, and set up monitoring systems for elections with new technology through the logical part of the brain, but we experience peace as well as war through the imaginative part of the brain. Through art, we often can learn to feel and to heal the trauma of killing. Who among us has not felt the power of war through Picasso's painting *Guernica* or the movie *Schlindler's List*? And as for peace, Jesus, our role model for peace, was, after all, a consummate storyteller.

S.H.

Poems

April 2008

Spring Seeds in a Time of War

by Elizabeth Schultz

The gutters retch
with wasted seeds.
Designed for renewal,
They lie in desiccated
mats on the hard land.
Too briefly, they
ornament the trees
with diverse contrivances
of pod and filamented catkin,
green and glorious
and blushing roseate.
Airborne, they fling
themselves outward
with acrobatic daring
Crossing boundaries
of yard and field
they die profligately.

April 2008

A Young Soldier Back from Iraq

by Lyn Back

He wore an Arab prayer shawl, cut off jeans,
The day he read his poems.
Back from Iraq. But not just back
Two years had passed since his return.
A boy of eighteen when he left. A boy.

Dark eyes beneath those heavy brows.
Beak nose, black shock of hair.
He looked down, then up, and frowned,
Stared at nothing I could see.
He looked like he was seeing ghosts. He was.

His clothes shook on his slender frame.
Legs trembling, he stood there.
We watched him take deep gulps of air.
Look out, raise up his chin and smile.
A brief, bright smile of who he once had been.

His voice boomed, roared. It slammed into me hard.
I felt the heat, the stench, his madness.
Exploding bodies, a fire storm, a blood letting of raw nerves.
He'd been a medic, a boy, eighteen years old.
His orders were, "Clean up this mess:" He isn't God.

His choking gasps filled up the silent room.
We didn't know what to do, or where to look
An older man, a vet, said something to him and they left.
Stood outside the door, locked in their tears. I thought,
"We do this. We do this. To our children."

December 2008

Epistemology

by Ed Higgins

It's always about loss,
this kind of epistemology
philosophers regard with dread.
And we can fool ourselves with thinking.
Like the grandfather
I read about recently
who picked up his four-year-old grandson
in two pieces on a Baghdad market street,
after a sudden car bomb there.
And then just yesterday grocery shopping,
concentrating on which broccoli florets to buy,
out of the corner of my eye
a little blond four-year-old girl
is running to the side of my leg
yelling grandpa, grandpa, we saw your car
in the parking lot and knew it was you.
And my son and his beautiful wife
are smiling an aisle away,
near the potatoes and sweet onions,
she holding their year-old daughter
on her hip the way mothers do.
And I'm so happy to see them all there
in one piece that I begin to cry,
like a foolish, foolish old man.

June 15, 1967

Dream: Antameruasiafricand

by Emily Israel

Sometimes I dream of Antameruasiafricand, the new world, where everyone is dying from spring fever or from overexposure to each other; where balloons, red and yellow, black and white, conspire to overthrow all dictators; where free speech is universal to the degree that Russians, Americans, Chinese, English, South Africans, Israelis, and Jordanians are so exhausted from talking that they cannot fight, and atomic bombs take it upon themselves to smother themselves; the new world in which cigarette companies replace tobacco with chocolate, in which scientists synthesize sunshine into a panacea for hunger, sickness, cold, fear, and ignorance; in which perfume is not gotten from bottled odors, but from forget-me-nots and magnolia trees; a renovated world whose people are socially concerned to the degree that the United Nations must pass laws regulating maximum hours of concern; whose long-haired beatnik protesters are invited to tea at the White House, the Kremlin, and Buckingham Palace at four; whose people join hands from Vladivostok to Kalamazoo, raise their eyes to the sky and whisper "peace."

February 2006

Memoir:
Threading Saffron Peace
Through the Gates

by Tom Goodridge

A silent peace walk led by saffron-robed Buddhist monks and interreligious leaders was to pass through Christo's and Jeanne Claude's "The Gates" in Central Park, in New York City. A gate passed through can mark a transition. Gates often exclude something. But these unattached gates seemed built to include. Like so many bold mushrooms, 7,503 saffron gates sprang up to live for only 16 days in the first U.S. public park. Some New Yorkers wondered why we permitted gates, even pretty ones, in the space that is reserved for nature. The Gates were offered as art, New York was assured, as a wave of saffron in a month that can be drab with winter. What can such art offer us; why did 750,000 people visit our cold and snowy park? These "unnecessary" gates caught the imagination of many locals and brought more out-of-towners to the park than any previous event on record. If these gates summoned so many and gathered us so tightly together—could we thread elusive peace through them?

The morning of February 21, 2005 found me nursing a cold. Three inches of fresh snow had fallen, the air was cold, and the sky was gray. Despite all this, I wanted to be a part of this walk and arrived an hour early. I asked a man distributing saffron leaflets at Fifth Avenue and 72nd Street, by the Park's Inventors Gate, if I could assist him. The leaflets read: "The Spirit of the Gates: a walking meditation through Christo's installation in Central Park. Presented by the Interfaith Center of N.Y., the Tricycle Foundation, and the N.Y. Buddhist Council." Since it didn't seem right to "hawk" a silent peace procession, I just held up the leaflets to passersby. They went slowly at first, but almost 100 were taken in the last 15 minutes. By the starting time, two o'clock, all the leaflets had gone; so I joined the swelling crowd of approximately 200 people. I discovered three friends in the throng; but our animated greetings were cut short by the sound of a wooden gong signaling the start of the journey. Temporarily halted at the initiatory gate, the crowd stood together braced against the cold. A few at a time were released through the narrow gate—released to wend their way through the saffron-marked path over the whitened land.

From the 16-foot-high gate frames of saffron-colored plastic hung nine feet of matching fabric. We passed under the seven-foot openings created under the flowing curtains. These ceremonial banners marked the two-mile route that led us up Cedar Hill and down again along the park's western side. The saffron color was also woven through the crowd, as many folks had found something in their wardrobe to match the color. Some of the monks that passed, from a variety of Buddhist orders, wore gray or burgundy garb—together we wove a bright tapestry on a misty afternoon. The walking was treacherous at times. Icy spots further slowed our meditative gait. Shared silence allowed our minds to roam as our feet followed the path. The fallow land seemed able to hold our thoughts even as it held the water of Turtle Pond, which we passed. My thoughts turned to other people from the United States, dressed in olive drab, patrolling the warmer, dryer Iraqi land, holding guns that demanded peace. We moved, disarmed, through the pastoral landscape of threading gates built just for joy. How could such disparate missions for peace ever be joined?

I was startled from my musings to find the face of a dear friend who had moved away many months ago. She and I had marched together in Washington, D.C., just before the bombing of Iraq. We were still marching, but now it seemed that we were moving toward peace rather than against war. Because we could not talk, I took her arm; two friends walked as one.

What will it take to get us through the gates of peace? Is peace born of idleness? Is it a byproduct of extravagance?—a criticism leveled at these gates. Was this peace walk an empty gesture—did it support only a peaceful fantasy? What did the other gate-watchers think as this procession of pilgrims plodded by? New Yorkers are not generally known as quiet, slow-moving folk eager to venture into nature on cold, gray winter afternoons. Had the desire for peace humbled them?

Without talk we were better able to observe the land. We passed a stream whose dark waters broke through a white slope descending from the Great Lawn. Our plodding, human bond had covered most of the two-mile course, bringing warm blood to frozen land. What will deliver the peace? How can we unite, despite our apparent differences, and bow our heads low enough to clear the gates of surrender? The walk ended with a brief interfaith service beside Cherry Hill, near the Park's Women's Gate, at Central Park West and 72nd St. Again the hollow wooden gong sounded.

About the Editor:

S haron Hoover is a longtime member of Alfred (N.Y.) Monthly Meeting, Farmington-Scipio (N.Y.) Regional Meeting, and New York Yearly Meeting. For Sharon, that has meant participating in many Quaker activities from First-day school to clerking and recording for local, regional, and yearly meetings. It has also meant camping with youth, singing around firesides, and sitting at bedsides. She has been blessed in sojourning in meetings in Santa Barbara, California; Missoula, Montana; Lincoln, Nebraska; and Ft. Lauderdale, Florida. Currently, she attends the Lewes Worship Group in Lewes, Delaware.

Sharon has been dedicated to finding ways to bring peace, a religious sense of life, and a deeper understanding and commitment to living in the communities around and beyond her since she was a child. She has enjoyed successes and learned humility from failures throughout her years of various responsibilities in the teaching profession and in raising a family and participating in her community. She is glad to have learned along the way that success and failure mean nothing. Seeking faithfully is the way.

Today, in learning "to hallow her diminishments," she is doing more service from her desk and less in public venues. She remains buoyed by the service and friendship of the many faithful Friends who have gone before her, who surround her now, and who seek to come after.

Most of all, she gives thanks to the Great Spirit of Creation.

www.ingramcontent.com/pod-product-compliance
Lightning Source LLC
Chambersburg PA
CBHW072148270326
41931CB00010B/1930